Massaging the Medium

Seven Pechakuchas

Language in Action Series

Adeena Karasick
Forest Hills, NY

INSTITUTE OF GENERAL SEMANTICS

Published by the Institute of General Semantics
72-11 Austin Street, #233
Forest Hills, New York, 11375
www.generalsemantics.org

Interior Book Design by Scribe Freelance
www.scribefreelance.com

ISBN: 978-1-970164-14-5 (Print)
978-1-970164-15-2 (eBook)
Published in the United States of America

Library of Congress Cataloging-in-Publication Data

Names: Karasick, Adeena, 1965- author.
Title: Massaging the medium : seven pechakuchas / Adeena Karasick.
Description: Forest Hills, NY : Institute of General Semantics, [2022] |
  Series: Language in action | Includes bibliographical references. |
  Summary: "Massaging the Medium consists of seven poetic probes and
  explorations of philosophical concepts regarding language, literature,
  media, technology, consciousness, and culture. Drawing inspiration from
  the field of media ecology and the discipline of general semantics, the
  text plays with language, and is accompanied by illustrations based on
  pechakucha presentations, here adapted for the print medium"-- Provided
  by publisher.
Identifiers: LCCN 2022005038 (print) | LCCN 2022005039 (ebook) | ISBN
  9781970164145 (paperback) | ISBN 9781970164152 (ebook)
Subjects: LCGFT: Visual poetry. | Experimental poetry.
Classification: LCC PR9199.3.K365 M37 2022 (print) | LCC PR9199.3.K365
  (ebook) | DDC 811/.54--dc23/eng/20220204
LC record available at https://lccn.loc.gov/2022005038
LC ebook record available at https://lccn.loc.gov/2022005039

The **Language in Action** series, sponsored by the Institute of General Semantics, publishes books devoted to creative modes of expression that can open the doors of perception, and foster better understandings of the nature of language, symbols, communication, and the semantic, technological, and media environments that we inhabit. Through processes of play and probing, art can bring into awareness alternative forms of experience and evaluation to the everyday, routine, taken-for-granted world. It can also shed new light on mind and method, consciousness and culture, abstracting and attention, ecology and enlightenment, and, most important to students of general semantics, science and sanity.

Founded in 1938 by Alfred Korzybski, the Institute of General Semantics promotes, in the words of S.I. Hayakawa, *the study of how not be a damn fool.* As a non-aristotelian system devoted to enhancing human potential, general semantics has inspired numerous novelists, poets, artists, musicians, and creative thinkers. General semantics today is devoted to explorations of meaning and the meaning of meaning, of metaphors and memes, archetypes and arts, symbols and signals, signs and significance, codes and ciphers, sense perception and sense-making, and the vast variety of ways of seeing, feeling, and thinking that humanity is heir to. The quarterly journal of the IGS, *ETC: A Review of General Semantics*, has been publishing essays, research, and literary work since 1943.

Other titles included in the Language in Action Series
Lance Strate, Series Editor

Strate, Lance (2020). *Diatribal Writes of Passage in a World of Wintertextuality: Poems on Language, Media, and Life (But Not as We Know It)*

Levinson, Martin H., with Photography by Katherine Liepe-Levinson (2020). *Signal Reactions and Other Poems*

Acknowledgments

I WOULD LIKE to thank Lance Strate (Fordham University) for his endless inspiration, as teacher, guide and muse over these past 7 years leading me into these explosive worlds; to Michael Plugh (Manhattan College), for introducing me to the form, to Jim Andrews for the use of his vispo work collaged in many of the slides, as well as bill bissett, Daniel. F Bradley, Gary Barwin, Judith Copithorne, Derek Beaulieu, bpNichol; to Frank London and Maria Damon who, with their profoundly encyclopedic thinking, were my continuous sounding boards; to Daniel J. Middleton and Naomi Middleton for their fierce editing and design of this volume; and to all the organizers of the universities, conferences, festivals and symposia who invited me to present this work: Gregory Betts, Lance Strate, Michael Plugh, Alan Golding, Marty Levinson, Robert Kasher, Corey Anton, Valerie V. Peterson, Ed Tywoniak, Anastacia Kurylo; and the Institute of General Semantics for their continuous love, dedication and support.

For Robert Kasher, in memoriam
and Safia Karasick Southey --

my loving guides
as i mapped the territories

Contents

Preface
'Fan-fare for the General Semanticist,'
Maria Damon

MASSAGING THE MEDIUM, like all of Adeena Karasick's work, performs an exuberant engagement with language's many delights. Here, in her latest volume, Karasick takes what has become a standard genre for high-info-density presentations–the pechakucha–and makes it a dazzling, multi-modal display of pleasure in the generative imperative of communication itself, in all its fulsome dimensions–it becomes an art form.

Form

For anyone still unfamiliar with the format, pechakucha –Japanese for "chitchat" –is a highly stylized presentation form that comprises a public speech accompanied by twenty slides for visual demonstration, each of which is shown for twenty seconds, while the speaker addresses their (his/her) topic. Initiated in 2003 by a pair of architects working in Japan, the format (trademarked and copyrighted, by the way, in true contemporary entrepreneurial style) has spread to encompass a world-wide enthusiasm for a story-telling/info delivery style that relies on the visual as much as, or even more than, on the verbal. The English equivalent, "chitchat," deriving from "chatter," itself echoic initially of bird sounds and then widened to include gossip, jabber or the clacking of teeth as a result of extreme cold, has an adrenalin quality to it, as if the putative superficiality of the content were over-ridden by its urgent affect, resulting in a heady sense of being taken into an intimacy with the subject matter and the storyteller both. The semantic content of the chitchat, such as it may be, is simply the medium by which this ephemeral intimacy is bruited, given form, momentarily embodied. The originators of the pechakucha form were thinly, indeed transparently, disguising serious professional information in a "fun," blithely speedy delivery format. But far from being simply a gush of unrestrained verbiage, the form relies on its tight, prescripted rhythm for maximum impact. Pechakucha is, ideally, a bombshell of luxuriant matter shimmying in a tight red dress, a marriage of minimalism and excess.

Content/Enter Adeena Karasick

The extreme constraint, the symmetry, and the *speed* of the format provides the kind of container within which a verbal artist like performance poet Adeena Karasick, known for her dazzling linguistic pyrotechnics on page and stage, truly thrives, as the propulsive energy that characterizes her writing and reading style is given sharper urgency for being trapped in a small temporal space, forcing her maximalist relationship to communication and meaning to burst into semantic overdrive (it is no accident that the phrase "all that is" is one of her most frequent formal connectors). The fireworks of puns and visual stimulation contained in this book is more than that: it is a bullet-train through a set of modern and contemporary theories of communication, linked and articulated under the aegis of "general semantics," charging vertically upward into a stratosphere of almost-graspable apprehensions. These seven *tours de force* of serious play celebrate meaning and unmeaning, communication and miscommunication, the happy errors/eros of semantic and sonic slippage, the glories of the im/p/precise. Don't overthink it, but yes do overthink it if to overthink is to revel in it, plunge into its infinite unfurling potentialities and don't deny a single one its due, riding, as Karasick does, a vibe, a wavelength, a swell of words, allowing it to carry us to its il/logical dissolution. Nod to the mass cultural references as you surf by!

A Bit of "Close Reading"

For example, when Karasick sings, "My language is alive with the sound of technology," in the first chapter, she is turning the telephone user's embodied experience with the telephone against/athwart the historically "*dis*embodied" nature of the telephone voice –that is, when the telephone was first introduced, it shocked by virtue of its ability to transport the sound of the speaker's voice far from its source, to emerge out of a mechanical device, the "receiver" –a mediumistic word if ever there was one. But as we all know, the receiver is hand-held to the ear (or, nowadays, nestled in the ear), thus reinscribing a different kind of physical intimacy from that of being in the presence of one's interlocutor –an intimacy that is arguably far more acute, more proximal, more embodied for being more internal. Moreover, the reference to the smash-hit musical film of the 1960s –"the hills are alive with the sound of music" –in which Julie Andrews as the young Maria von Trapp, hurling her hymns to the hills in her pristine British warble while whirling about in an Alpine idyll, rubs up with comedic glee against contemporary theories of cyborg hybridity and the porousness of the very concept of "natural language." Thus, in one playful détournement, Karasick shows how the machinic and the organic are never in opposition, not even separate in their interactions, but symbiotic parts of an unlimited organism that could be called "the real," "life," "consciousness," or even our corporeo-linguistic imaginations.

And yes, "*a refracted parataxis, axioms of wracked praxis*" actually means something! Parsing one of Karasick's signature bits of sprezzatura reveals a solid theoretical basis for what may appear to be merely vaudevillian pastiche. To wit: Parataxis is a rhetorical ploy, a means of narrative whereby the standard semantic "connective tissue" of sentences and paragraphs –transitional and relational devices ("therefore," "thus we can see that," "as a result of," etc.), the small signals that create relations by subordinating one clause to another, or that develop a logic of causation or sense of dialectical narrative "progress" –are suppressed in favor of a more egalitarian adjacency: para + taxis = ordering through adjacency. Thus, "The king is dead. Long live the king" instead of "Although the elderly king has died, the category of kingship is transcendent, so his son will now ascend to occupy the position thus ascertaining that there is never *not* a king." *Refracted* means redirected; *wracked*, subject to extreme conditions or processes. As it appears in "Ceci N'est Pas Une Telephone or Hooked on Telephonics: A Pata-philophonemic Investigation of the Telephone," the *praxis* in question indicates extreme forms of experimentation, including scission –the telephone cuts and connects, facilitates both distance and intimacy. This is also, as is every topic announced by the chapter titles, a meta-commentary on Karasick's own preoccupations, praxes and pronouncements. Karasick tells you how to read her as she tells you how to read modern semantic phenomena in all their perplexity and wonder. Her sense of endless wonder is contagious, so let yourself be carried along by the murmuring waters of McLuhan, Derrida, Zizek, Benjamin and other ministering angels.

Fan-fare for the General Semanticist

In one of the most famous of many interrogations of the concept of authorship arising from the cerebral fever of the post-structural 1960s and 70s, to which Karasick is clearly indebted, Michel Foucault wrote, citing the minimalist Samuel Beckett, "What does it matter who is speaking?" Foucault was writing in the spirit of democratization, a challenge to the gate-keeping "author function" through which a process of selection creates a canonical hierarchy. Karasick plays her part in helping to level that hierarchy. In and through Karasick's text, everybody, every non-body, and every hybrid of embodied and disembodied, organic and inorganic matter, speaks, whispers, croons, warbles, ululates, whoops, natters, orates and babbles. The one element missing in this printed text lavish with optical and lexical pleasures is that of the embodied performance of Karasick herself, in person and limited by definable spatial/temporal co-ordinates, at the conferences where these pechakuchas took place. These chapters are, however, not mere simulacra or second-order evidentiary paper trails. What they lack in sentience they compensate for in inscrypted sentences and fragments as well as deliciously playful visual montages –they are both the detritus and the ultimate flowering of the "live performances." Strap on your seatbelt, readers, and taste her voice in your ear.

Introduction

I HAVE ALWAYS been obsessed with language; language as a technology; a prime mover in the re-distribution of aesthetic values. Whether on the page, the stage, the mise-en-scène, the screen, over my 35 years of publication and performance, the work draws on a range of neo Fluxus, post L=A=N=G=U=A=G=E, Sound Poetry, Concrete poetry and Vispo modes. And through an aesthetics of *jouiss-ey* transgression, invasion, contradiction, ambiguity, ornament, excess, heterogeneity, paradox, hybridity and desire, I have always been rapt with the physicality, materiality of language, how it sounds, looks, feels and tastes and the various ways meaning can be constructed from non-traditional modes of language construction -- and how that fundamentally affects the way we see, breathe, feel and act. How it propels us to see the world in new ways -- of parsed plays laced socio-political-lingual cultural shards, pulsing with palimpsested resonance; instruments of change with time-binding capacities.

As such, all the work is marked by a kind of intertextatic syntacticism; or in Korzybskian terms, "semantic disturbances," weaving meaning through questions and celebration, reverberation, elation, navigating ways this engagement with language invites us to embrace the impossibility of the possible, the contingency of our finitude, our brokenness, excess and exuberance, within the fissures of being.

. . .

In 2012, while teaching Communication and Media Studies at Fordham University, where Lance Strate was Program Director, I was introduced to a Japanese form of presentation by my then officemate, Michael Plugh. Originating in Tokyo, the word "pechakucha" (Japanese for *chitchat*) has been traditionally used as a mode for sharing often comedic, emotionally wrought, visually compelling stories. However, as a border, blurring, boundary busting Kabbalistically enmeshed, language-focused media ecological, general semanticist poet, I was infatuated with the idea of taking this form (20 slides, each one advances after 20 seconds, allowing for 20 seconds of live performance per slide, for 6 minutes and 40 seconds total), and re-choreographing it through a neo-formalist approach of reflection, deflection, refraction and the fracturing of language and image. And with a maximalist aesthetics, explore the relational contingencies of visual and acoustic space. Simultaneously foregrounding the physicality, materiality of language and image while delivering a live "talk" that blurs academic and poetic language, it asks the receiver to not only think about the subject matter but to negotiate the multiplicitous modes of information when conflictual communication models are at play; how and in what ways is the media massaging the message as it hits various emotional, psychological and cognitive registers at once.

Like Wittgenstein's generated aphorisms, Spinoza's numbered propositions, Heidegger's compound neologisms or Plato's dialogues, I was interested in using this form as a driving apparatus and exploding its parameters. And, as such, does not offer an analytic approach which asks and resolves problems in a clear and "transparent," delineated way, one which privileges clarity and closure but rather as a non-Aristotelian transpoesis -- of infractions, contractions, extractions, frictions, inscriptions, encryptions embedded with aporia, paradox, chiasms, curtains, covets and foregrounds its caveats.

This book *is based on* the pechakucha presentations but have been transformed into something new. Reworked, revised, reformed, recruited, redone, reordered, reformatted, rewritten, reconfigured, remediated, erupting as a new art form in which the original hybrid of oral and electronic media has been transformed into a written and printed form. Thus, technically and for the sake of accuracy, what is printed here are not *actually* pechakuchas but an adaptation and asks one to revisit and recontextualize, reframe information thinking through how the media indeed reshapes the message. In a kind of echopoeic transversal of McLuhan's epochs, it explodes into a post-electronic-age re-inscription; re-futuring print media – from "Gutenberg Galaxies" to a Gambiting Gal-lexes; mapping new territories.

And as such, as philosophically rigorous, poetically-inflected lines of inquiry, which are beyond *and* beside their original form, perhaps these pechakuchas might be more aptly named 'patakuchas – read through a Jarry-esque 'pataphysical framework, (the Science of Imaginary Endings, providing answers to questions never been asked).

So, whether it be a socio-historical re-investigation of the telephone
as an ever-evolving media apparatus; an examination of the
politics of "Imagination"; a general semanticist / media
ecological study of the apocryphal figure of Salomé;
a transpoetic re-navigation of ways in which
Postman's "Crazy Talk, Stupid Talk" can
be read through contemporary poetry and
poetics; a cross-cultural, interdisciplinary
study of how Conceptual Poetry intersects
with McLuhan ideologies; a rereading of the work
of Canadian poet, painter, concrete and sound artist,
bill bissett through both a Kabbalistic and Korzybskian lens;
or thinking through a history of "talking media" as represented
through pop culture, underscoring ways the ghost is literally in the machine --

through a re-mapping of acoustic and visual space, and a border-blurring subverted mode of academic discourse, these pechakuchas intermediatically play through intertextual polyvalence, puns and ellipses, defractions, transpositions, "contrascriptions," erupting as a landscape of influences, filiations, legacies all labyrinthine and abyssal; erupting perhaps as how Luce Irigaray (in *Marine Lover*) describes "woman" – a plurality gathered into a matrix of interrelations. A kind of "annextual discourse," a series of McLuhanesque probes.

The medium allowed me exquisite axes of entry into a virtual arena where not only can the materiality of language be exposed, but through the conflagration of image, music, voice, text, sound and animation, it highlights a 'textatic' slipperiness of meaning. And each piece, operating with its own structure, codes, logic, idioms, reminds us how meaning-making is always a praxis of palimpsest and dissemination, generating a contiguous infolding of meaning.

Originally these pieces were created for and presented from 2013-2019, at academic literary conferences, including the 42nd Annual Louisville Conference On Literature & Culture Since 1900, University of Louisville, Louisville, Kentucky, *TEXT/SOUND/ PERFORMANCE: Making in Canadian Space,* University College Dublin, Dublin, Ireland; the Institute of General Semantics symposiums held in conjunction with the 61st, 62nd, 63rd, 64th, 65th, and 66th annual Alfred Korzybski Memorial Lecture and Symposium; The 14th Annual Media Ecology Association Convention; The 71st, 72nd, 74th and 75th Annual New York State Communication Association conferences; The 104th Eastern Communication Association Convention, and Book Expo America, 2014 as part of "The Media IS the Message: Multi-Media and the Future of Publishing" with Ralph Rivera, BBC Future Media; in New York, Providence, Michigan, Callicoon, Louisville, Ellenville and Dublin.

And though these 7 pechakuchas re-map a wide range of territories, each are underscored with an obsession with language itself – with ways language creates being, as manifested most overtly with the appearance and reappearance of the Golem, and in the bissett-focused, *Chants Rattles and Trance* (or *the Non-Allness of Abstraction*), even provides the instructions to construct one as laid out in Kabbalistic doctrine. A further focus that runs through many of these pieces are my passion for juxtaposing "high" and low cultural markers – so in both the visuals and the text there is a *jouissey* mix that erupts as a luxuriously non-dichotomous synchrony of affect. Another significant strand that weaves through each piece, is a negotiating of the difficult notion of truth construction and its ever-elusiveness but yet how it's so politically crucial to acknowledge how and in what ways it's unveiling and veiling in simulation, dissimulation, secrets of a secret that only another secret can unveil -- never just a free flow of indiscriminate information but is always already contextual and must be woke to its foundations, fabrications; grounded maybe in what Derrida might call, a chordal "accord or concord of correspondences."

And as you can't take the jew out of the *jouissance*, each pechakucha erupts as an analytic meditation on the relationship between language, culture, technology and communication, bound by a firm commitment to play and *plaisir*. Incorporating a hyper-generative aesthetics highlighting recycled language, sampling, borrowing, cutting, pasting, mash-up; engaged in an 'inter-ventive' poetics marked by neo-formalized post-consumerist media-infused transgressive linguistic practices – underscoring how whether on or off the screen, each luxuriant reference, phrase, meme is saturated with ideological codes, intertextually drenched palimpsested systems, an ever-shifting political, social, gendered logospace of 'ambi-valence'.

. . .

Ceci n'est pas un Télé-phone or Hooked on Telephonics: A 'Pata-Philophonemic Investigation of the Telephone is a playfully, politically historic reckoning with the telephone; its uses and associations; how it's both transformed over time and transformed our lives. Responding to McLuhan's, 1964, *Understanding Media: Extensions of Man,* predicting not only that the Internet would become a "global village" that will retribalize us and cause us to be more interconnected than television, this pechakucha explores ways the telephone has shifted our sense of time and space, orders, borders, closes the gap between producers, consumers, creators; how it truly is "an extension of our bodies."

Continuing with the notion of disruption of time, space and reality, *Where **is** Fancy Bred: Rethinking Imagination Through the "Unthought" and How that Affects Communication* thinks through "Imagination" from both a 'pata etymologic and playfully deconstructive lens, renegotiating it through both academia and pop culture markers. It investigates ways for example, like how for Lacan and Zizek, the imaginary (between the symbolic and the real) *is* where identity unfolds; the site of the formation of the ego: *i-mago*. Always already an image of an image, thinking though the imagination, reminds us how the real reels in irreality surreality, a seriality of slippery surfaces endlessly signifying; an homage'nation or immersion'ation of links, subversions, excursions, perversions.

The multiply titled: *The Ghost is In the Machine: Medium, Messages and Mysticism*, originally titled, *Back in the O.S. Back in the O.S. Back in the O.S.V.R or Siriusly? Medium, Messages and Mysticism: Binding Time with your OS* explores the relationship between technology, language and spirituality in contemporary media. With reference to pop cultural manifestations of the Disembodied Voice, as in Spike Jonez', Her or Apple's, Siri as a 21st Century Golem, it highlights how the mystical and the machine are not oppositional, but that "all media are extensions of man that cause deep and lasting changes and transform our environment" (McLuhan) and opens not a physical vs metaphysical, but 'pataphysical space reminding us how language and thereby all knowledge is spectral, virtual, simulacric.

The Crazy Talk of Checking In is a Postmanic 'pata semantic reinvestigation of what Postman termed "Crazy Talk / Stupid Talk," exposing how the language of "poetry" can address some of these issues. It includes a selection from my 2018 book, *Checking In* and in live performance was accompanied by the deliciously complex video by Jim Andrews, which takes over 700 images referencing the text and mashes them up, ironically celebrating language that is "irrational," "confused," "decontextualized" and "distorted."

Composed at the height of the Conceptual Poetry craze, *Medium in a Messy Age: Communication in the Era of Technology* tracks through some of the major players, concepts and strategies of Conceptual Poetry, and its socio-historic, aesthetic and political underpinnings. With shout outs to Christian Bök's, *Xenotext Experiment*, Kenny Goldsmith, Rob Fitterman's, pop-up Word shop, Craig Dworkin's *Parse*, Sound poetry, Concrete poetry, Conceptual Poetry's cousin Flarff, and read through Benjamin, Burroughs, Battailles Baudrillard, Pound, Kittler, Mallarmé, the Dadaists and Surrealists, it's a playful media ecological investigation of Conceptual Poetry and its impact on communication.

Continuing this focus on poetry as a politically crucial mode of meaning production, between McLuhan's notion of Acoustic Space and T.S. Eliot's Auditory Imagination, Korzybski's "In-Sanity" and the ancient Kabbalistic practice of Golem construction, *Maps and Terrortories, PreScience and In-Sanity: bill bissett and the Non-Allnes of Abstraction* navigates some of the uncanny intersections, overlaps and trajects between Canadian poet, painter and sound artist bill bissett and both media ecologic and general semanticist concepts; exposes ways his sound work resounds as a "coefficient causality," where effect begets effect in an erratic praxis of socio-political mystical and secular vectors, through a synnexes of lexis, excess, access and fracturous raptures and underscores language's profound power for transformation and change.

Digging deeper into the transformative powers of language, accentuated by a range of intermediatic modes – as a literal technoVERSE, the final pechakucha in this edition draws on my extensive research surrounding the myth of the apocryphal figure of Salomé. Situated between the expanding boundaries of text and textuality, sound experiments, sonic spaces, and performance, *Scenes, Screams, Screens, and Semes: The Salomaic Elasticity of the Page and the Stage* contextualizes *Salomé: Woman of Valor*, my 2018 Spoken Word Opera which revisits the apocryphal figure of Salomé through a Jewish feminist lens. As a book (published in an English/Italian bi-lingual edition by University of Padua Press and in Bengali as *Salome Birangona*, an English-only libretto by Gap Riot Press in Toronto, CD (NuJu Records, New York, 2020) *and* a performance piece, it negotiates a range of revolutionary intersections – not only in the integration of styles and traditions, between poetry, midrash, Kabbalah and pop culture, highlighting polyphonic textures and rhythmic wordplay, but how this manifests when filtered through various media. Through both form and content, it exposes how narrative is always mutiperspectival and slippery; ex-statically palimpsested – celebrating the porous aporia between the *vois, vuel, voile, veux, voila*; hearing and seeing, seeing and saying, essaying as Walter Ong says, "I see what you say. But what we are seeing is not what we are saying."

All syllogistically exilic, juxtaposing a range of communicative strategies: between poetry, prose, aphorism, pop culture and prayer, philosophic idioms, syllogisms and slang; the voice, the page, the stage, the screen, these pieces highlight ways messages are massaged *through* media; how they play in the interstices, the spaces between mediums; between the eye and the ear, orality, aurality, echographies, ways language and meaning are differently received, and how language opens itself as a place of contemplative hunger -- for new ways of thinking and thereby being; and the anti-hegemonic possibilities that arise from such an engagement.

The visuals consist of both found and original collaged material which both speak to and against the text. And each of the original slides were embedded with audio and video clips, gifs, other forms of kinetic digital media such as montages of sound poetry from bill bissett, Steve McCaffery, Paul Dutton, Christian Bök in *Medium in a Messy Age,* as well as a clip of Kenny Goldsmith reading from *Traffic* at the White House and my ironic re-translation of Beyoncé's 2008 hit, "Single Ladies," "Lingual Ladies." *The Crazy Talk of Checking In* pechakucha included a montage of pop songs highlighting the word "Crazy" and "Stupid" (ie "Still Crazy After All These Years," "She Drives me Crazy," "Crazy on You," "Let's Go Crazy," "Dare to Be Stupid," "She Talk Crazy Talk.") *The Ghost is In the Machine* pechakucha included a montage of horror film clips highlighting talking media: with shout-outs to *The Car, Poltergeist, Blade Runner*, Videodrome, *Her* and *Dr. Who.* The *Imagination* pechakucha featured a mashup of *Willy Wonka's*, "A World of Pure Imagination," John Lennon's, "Imagine," Gary Wright's, "Dream Weaver," Gladys Knight and the Pips', "I've Got to Use My Imagination," and the Pretenders', "...gonna use my, my, my imagination..." *Ceci n'est pas un Télé-phone* included a mashup of audio and visual clips of songs relating to telephones including Laurie Anderson's, "Hello I'm not Here Right Now," Blondie's, "Call Me," Tommy Tutone's, "867-5309/ jenny," Stevie Wonder's, "I just called to say..." and Beyoncé and Lady Gaga's, "Telephone." What is illustrated here, however are stills from the digital live motion presentation, and although originally all consisting of 20 separate components, they are now of slightly varying length.

Through a series of excesses, accesses, anguishes, fragilities, agilities, as a ventriloquized latticework, each frame erupts, in the words of Anne Blonstein, as a kind of contaminative "lexicell," exaltically and ecstatically dis-easing the form, a way a virus might enter another's DNA, erupting as a consanguinity of inter-constellated contingencies. And in general semanticist terms, enacts a sense of "time binding," speaking to the ever-cyclic / spiraling nature of meaning and being.

And like McLuhan's, Laws of Media whereby an artifact enhances, reverses, retrieves and obsolesces, each pechakucha re-visits concepts and are re-contextualized through a Jewish, feminist, post-structural, semiotic re-reading. In Zoharic terms, (13th C. mystical discourse), they employ the concept of *atikin haditin,* a pseudo-Aramaic neologism that means "ancient new." Journeying nomadic and vagrant, deep within an ancient form, and in Pound's lexicon "makes it new." Through multi-sensoric polyvocal play of ocular and acoustic space, it summons its reader (whether they be media ecologists, general semanticists, communication theorists or literary scholars), to rethink notions of language, technology and meaning production --

to open each piece like an open letter
an *envoi* that travels through lexical textures
eruptions, corruptions, chambers, crevices, debts
and accountabilities to ever-wandering destinations.

. . .

As titles and contents of the pieces were often "massaged" for the various venues, below is a complete listing of their names, dates and presentation locations.

- *Ceci n'est pas un Télé-phone* or *Hooked on Telephonics: a 'Pata-Philophonemic Investigation of the Telephone* as part of *"Multi-media futures and other New Dimensions for Publishing and Content Dissemination"* for BookExpo America 2013, Javitz Center, New York, NY; and the 14th Annual Convention of The Media Ecology Association, Grand Valley University, Grand Rapids, Michigan, 2013, and the audio featured on St. Rocco's Broadcast for the Dispossessed, WCAA 107.3, Dec. 5, 2021.

- *Where **is** Fancy Bred? Rethinking Imagination Through the "Unthought" and How That Affects Communication for the 64th Alfred Korzybski Memorial Lecture* and Symposium: Language in Thought and Action, Institute of General Semantics, Princeton Club, New York, NY, 2016. Originally presented as "Journey of the (I)magi: The Imajouissance of Communication Theory" for the 74th Annual Conference (Imagination), New York State Communication Association Conference, Villa Roma Resort & Conference Center, Callicoon, NY, Oct. 15, 2016.

- *The Ghost is In the Machine: Medium, Messages and Mysticism*, originally titled, *Back in the O.S. Back in the O.S. Back in the O.S.V.R or Siriusly? Medium, Messages and Mysticism: Binding Time with your OS.* for Book Expo America, 2014 as part of "The Media IS the Message: Multi-Media and the Future of Publishing" (with Ralph Rivera, BBC Future Media); the 72nd New York State Communication Association Conference and the 62ndAlfred Korzybski Memorial Lecture and Symposium for the Institute of General Semantics, New York, NY, 2014. Medium in a Messy Age: Communication in the Era of Technology (alternatively subtitled: The Media Ecology of Conceptual Poetry), for the 71st Annual New York State Communication Association Conference and the 61st Alfred Korzybski Memorial Lecture symposium for the Institute of General Semantics, New York, NY, 2013.

- *Refracted Facts: The Crazy Talk of Checking In: A Postmanic 'Pata Semantics*, originally titled *Refracted Facts in the Holes of Oblivion: The 'Crazy Talk' of Checking In* for the 65th Alfred Korzybski Memorial Lecture symposium for the Institute of General Semantics, New York, NY, 2017; and *Re-mything History: Honoring the Past, Shaping the Future* for the New York State Communication Association 75th Annual Conference Callicoon, NY, 2017.

- *Maps and Terrortories, PreScience and In-Sanity: bill bissett and the Non-Allnes of Abstraction* at the 63rd Alfred Korzybski Memorial Lecture symposium: Language and "Reality" Institute of General Semantics, The Princeton Club, New York, NY, Oct. 2015. Originally presented as *Chants Rants Rattles and Trance: bill bissett and the KaBABEListics of Acoustic Space,* for the 42nd Annual Louisville Conference on Literature & Culture Since 1900, University of Louisville, Louisville, KY, Feb. 2015.

- *Scenes, Screams, Screens, and Semes: The Salomaic Elasticity of the Page and the Stage* was presented for *TEXT/SOUND/ PERFORMANCE: Making in Canadian Space,* University College Dublin, Dublin, Ireland, April 25, 2019. Originally appeared as *Bandage, Bondage, Strippers and Slippage: The Language and Meaning of Salomé in the 21st Century* for the 66th Alfred Korzybski Memorial Lecture symposium: "Language and Meaning in the 21st Century" Institute of General Semantics, New York, NY, 2018.

Ceci N'est Pas Une Telephone

or

Hooked on Telephonics
A Pata-philophonemic Investigation of the Telephone

It is time to speak of the voice that touches--
always at a distance, like the eye – and the telephone caress,
if not the (striking) phone call[1]

1

In *Understanding Media*, Marshall McLuhan calls the telephone
"speech without walls," "an extension of the ear."
But "as the sender is sent," somewhere over the Verizon,
it's not just an ear, say
but a full-on sensorium of screening memes and flashy apps,
my telephone is my phonebook, tv, newspaper,
cinema, menu, library, my living room

As the old Bell slogan used to say, "Reach Out and Touch Someone,"
the telephone is a tactile medium.
For Derrida, "When I speak to you, I touch you…from however far off
[] you're your voice's inflection on the telephone."[2]
But between touching and the untouchable,
with our high def flat-panel two-tone track-tap touch screens,
there is an "absolute" untouchability

3

According to Freud, the telephone is a connecting of the unconscious
through the receiver[3]. But if the receiver is the caller[4] and a call is a caress
the telephone is caressing the unconscious:

Not just a telephone but
a troll-a-phone, a tag-a-phone of re-tallied tumblr telos
of inimitable, illimitable, sub-liminal thresholds
where my unconscious is touching your unconscious.

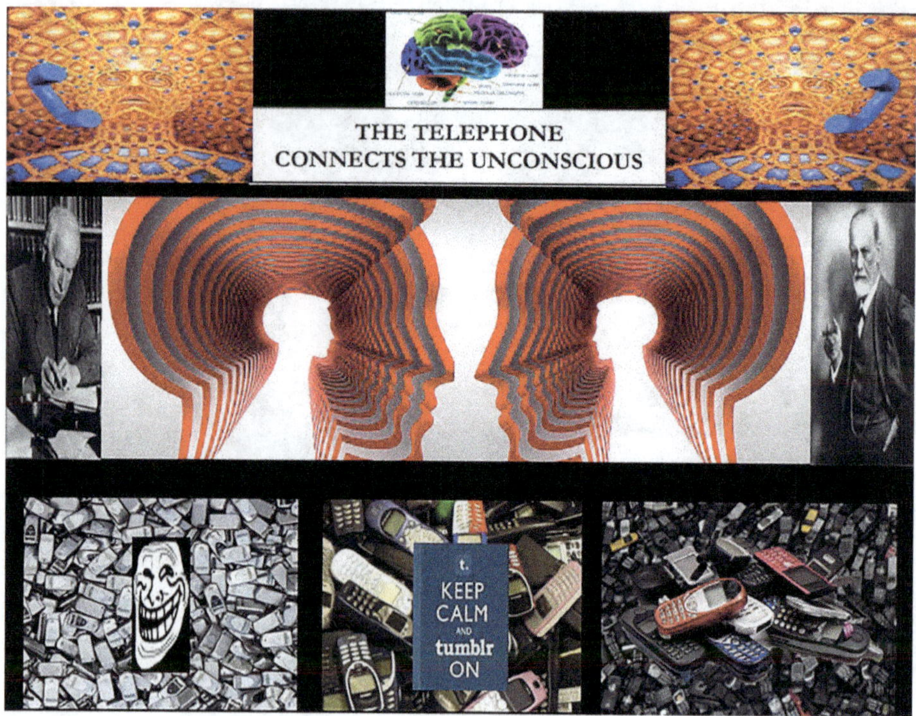

4

The telephone is prosthetic and foregrounds the amputative present
metonymic of meaning production itself. Reminding us
that no matter how sophisticated the media,
the message never fully arrives.

All static-y in a-semic dyssemia,
there's always (as Shannon might say), "noise in the system."[5]
All dirty n distorted, something always
gets lost in transmission.

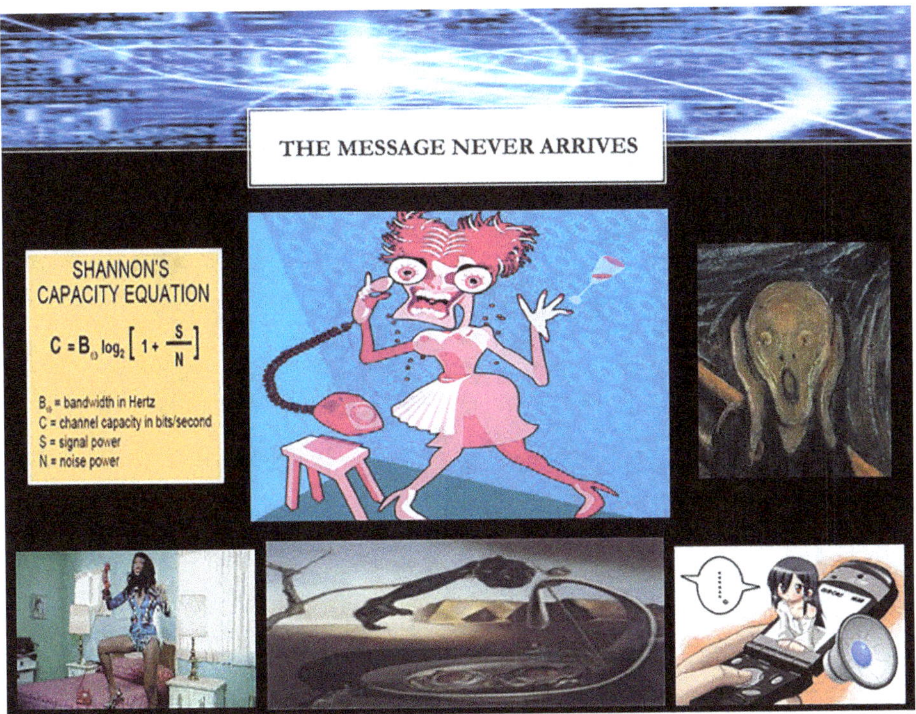

And as we are re-mediated through now wireless technologies
the present is always re-presented in a messy prescience,
a pressing sense that the future of the future
is the present which we walk backwards into; a present
(which is also a gift) a *gif* given with no giver, re-gifted
in a re-mediated immediacy

6

And though this immediacy is at times phenomenal
through an endless barrage of alerts,
it [c]ells us a sense of ersatz significance;
is a source of endless distraction, thwarts our ability to focus,
reflect, analyze, filter or synthesize information,

yet has become a site of toxic addiction.

Proust calls the telephone a "supernatural instrument"[6]
through which we make the non-present present
through the other's vocal inflections, timbres, accents,
cultivating a spectral phantasm,
a [f]antasmatic specter foregrounding
how the word "phony" also means "unreal voice." [7]

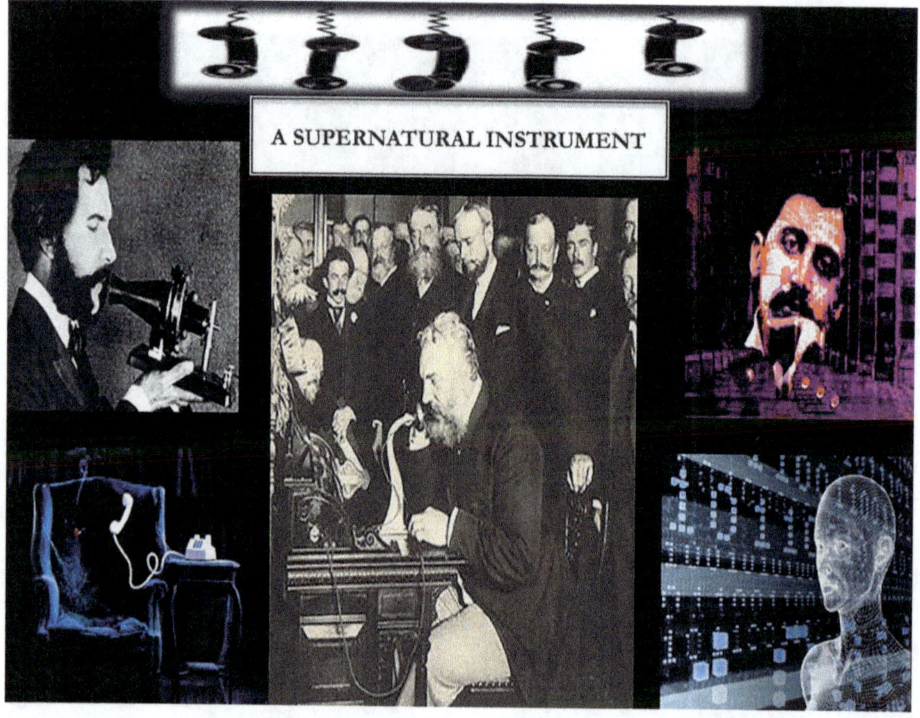

Or just as Kern argues, the telephone fundamentally alters
our understandings of time and space;
the telephone enables us to "be in [multiple] places at the same time"[8]
annihilates distances, "expands lived space,"
where all is re-*plaised* in hyper-spatial interplays.
Remembering that an early definition of cyberspace is
"where you are when you talk on the phone."[9]

9

And as i use my telephone to not just speak to but to message, text,
WhatsApp Meta tumblr twitter you, it becomes synechdochic
of where grammatology meets orality.

My language is alive with the sound of technology
and thus kicks some age old Western teleological binaric distinction
to the curb giving PHONE-CENTRISM a new meaning.

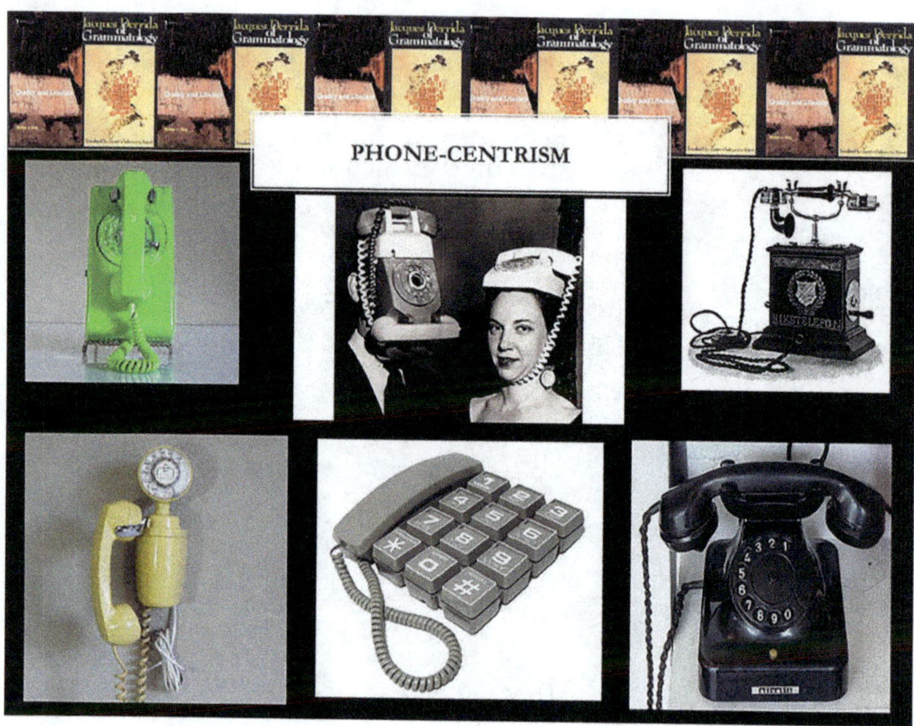

10

Because even though *phone* means *sound*, as in phonetics,
it comes from the ancient Greeks, who adapted the Semitic alphabet
referring to it as Phoenician writing.[10]

So, with both my mouth and my fingers, i participate in my media
re-signing sounds through new symbolic systems of
m-m-my telephone

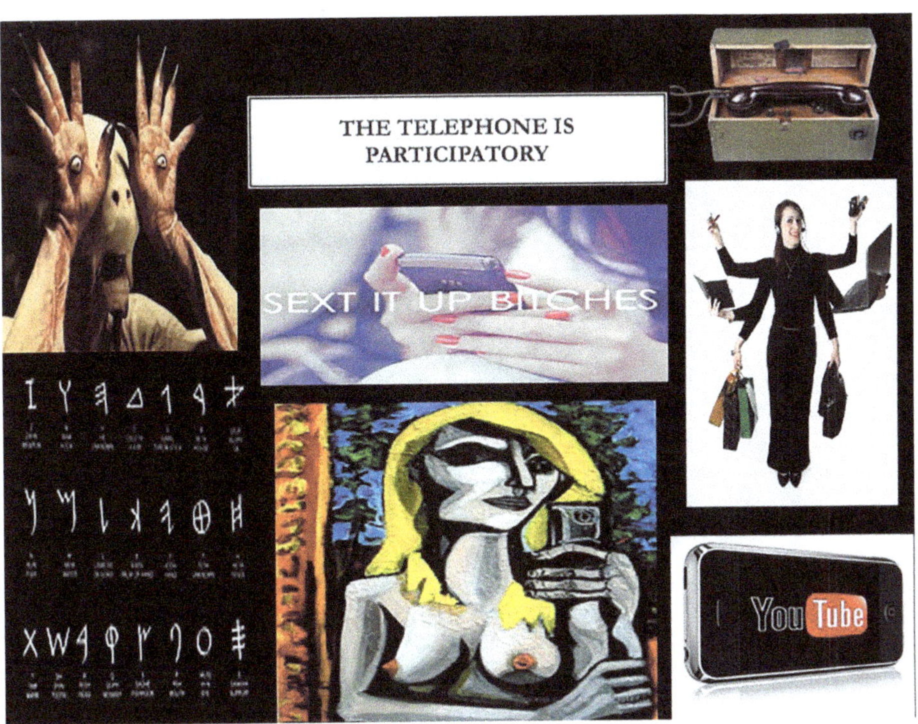

which à la Katy Perry, is both HOT and it's COLD,
in and it's out. Thus, not just updating the McLuhan axiom but
represents the mark of Derridean circumcision.[11]
The telephone *is* the cut that opens the word or the heart
or the ear of the other; both a cutting *off* and *into*;
a refracted parataxis, axioms of wracked praxis.

12

And as it arouses sight, and touch, and even smell,[12]
the telephone becomes aTikTokin' iPadded Galaxy,
a Zoomalicious Google-Meet tweetin'
global village; a cordless cord of entwined bodies
imposing a ventriloquy, not just separating the voice from the body,
the body from being but connecting and reconnecting
through an orgiastic arena of linkages.

13

And as such, all rechargeable and wireless,
the telephone allows us as hunters and gatherers,
to re-roam the world as modern nomads.[13]
Unattached and unencumbered by maps, compass, books,
cameras, CDs, but can freely traverse, vagrant
knowing we are never alone.

i wander only as a crowd.

According to McLuhan, the term "telephone" originated in 1840 and first referred to "a device made to convey musical notes through wooden rods."[14] And it was the little-known Philippe Reis in the 1860's who produced the first "musical telephone"[15] foregrounding the relation between the media and its messages embedded in its very definition.

So, whether it's Blondie's, "Call me," or Tommy Tutone's, "Jenny 867 5309," Stevie Wonder's, "I just called to say, I love you," or ELO's, "Hello, how are you, Have you been all right," Chuck Berry's, "Memphis girl" who "could not leave her number" or Gaga's, "Sorry I can't hear you. I'm K-kinda Busy," the telephone has been featured in music throughout history, foregrounding the angst of disconnection.

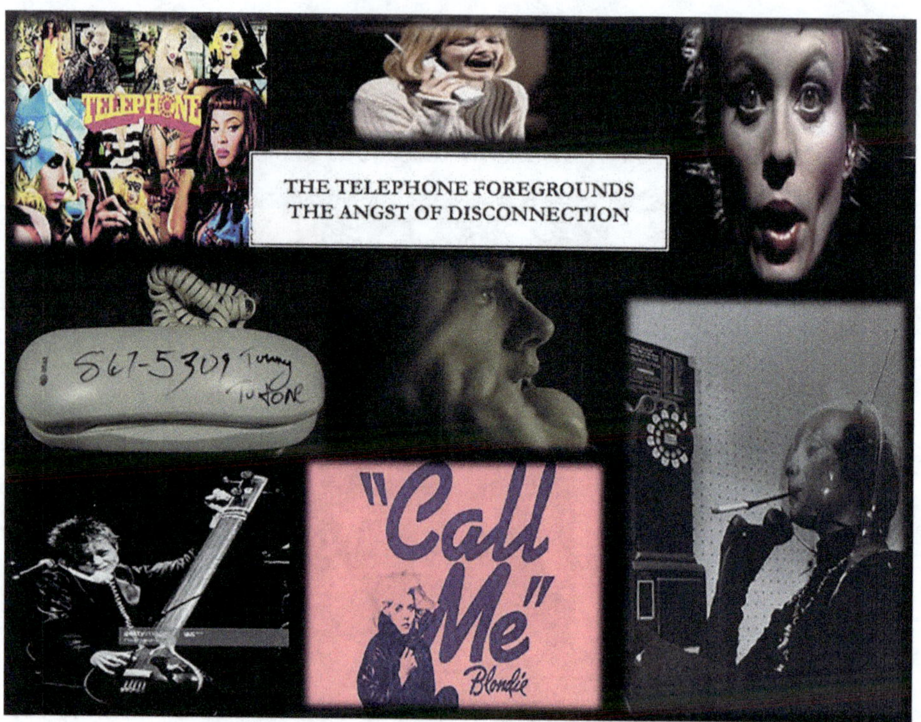

16

And through intraphonemic telephony, you can "Call me Maybe"[16]
but my real name is [] intertextual --
as Derrida points out in *Ulysses Gramaphone*;
showing how the telephone connects all possible narrative
and signifying lines of communication.[17] The telephone
like a Prophet, is the network through which all information
is transmitted.

But that information, like in the children's game, "Telephone"
is often distorted. And though the telephone
is used to spread information,
lines are crossed, and it becomes a tattlephone a tale-a phone, detailing
and retelling as the tell tolls.

As Avital Ronnel might say, destabilizes subjectivity;
connecting the un-connectable.[18]

18

The telephone shows us how "technology has broken into the body."
Cronos-style, we are "tele–Vaccinated,"[19]
injected with otherness, as the telephone provides
a fanatically addictive portal into
the ear of the other. Piercing our skin:
our wallskin, gameskin, brainskin, mindskin
skimming the screens of our cells
which are bifurcating.

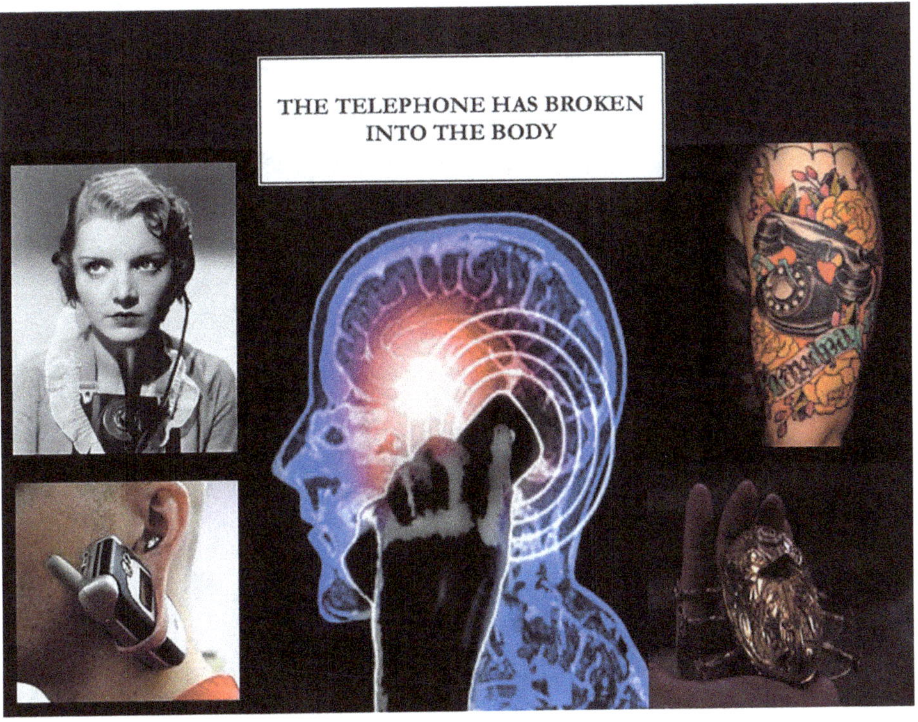

Thus, the telephone foregrounds how we are all 'schizophrenic'
multiple and uncontainable. How language itself
as a mediated technology,
is always inscribed in excess, abundance, interruption, disruption
mute-ated in a polyglossic heresay of voice-overs, mirrors, screens,
memes, mimes, memories, murmuring
through an infinite untranslatability.

20

And, as we traverse our Insta TikTok Snapchat Apple-mapped
cell-poppin' technoverse, grafting phantasms, images
trying to connect;
the *tele* (far away) and the *phone* (voice)
bringing a sense of immediacy of presence, being
the telephone can never be understood as *das ding*
(a thing–in–itself), but represents a thinking
that responds and recalls.

And literally responding, as my shockingly bright, smart phone
embedded with chips, keys, tracks, mines, monitors --
through salient valence, surveillance,
trailing, detailing unveiling, *re-mailing*
now tells me "what i want what i really, really want"

As a communicative technology, is itself communicating.

22

Thus, all webbed up, beaten down, slap-appy and high def,
triggered tweeting, trending images on the galaxy walls
the telephone reminds us that however tribally connected
we think we are --

through social dizziness, a scrambling of relations,
it's also increasingly dividing us –

And, if in Hebrew the "c[l]all" is the awareness of the underlying unity
that makes the individual a part of a people, the telephone is
"c[l]alling" upon us
to re-think ritual, association, membership, mediums, environments,
identity and the c[a]llective

as an ever ringing *das ding* of open secrets
through the intertubes of meaning, live streaming
screaming to be heard

Where Is Fancy Bred?
Rethinking Imagination Through the "Unthought" and How That Affects Communication

"Because we can imagine we are ontologically free" (Sartre)

1

Throughout history, literature, philosophy, general semantics and media ecology, the imagination is the region of the possible; embodying all that is fanciful, virtual and full of desire. But, read through Hellenistic antiquity, Indo-European or Sanskrit etymology, *magos, maya, mag(h)* it embodies the power *to act*. Thus, embedded within its very name, "to imagine" is to make real.

Re-read through Heidegger and Edmond Jabès' notion of the "unthought" (the inner horizon of thought), and Lacan, as a site of "unconscious organization," where all is sampled, juxtaposed, imagination; an emerge'nation, a merger'nation -- an *enjambination*; germinating the interval of all that is uncharted.

'cause inside "ima**gin**ation" is *en-gyn*, not just that which is spectral, magical and fanciful but the "work work work work work work"[20] a complex of interlocuted loci, a colloquy of connections, synnexions, predilections. The imagination, an i-*machination*, or for Deleuze, Guattari and Lacan, "an interpretive machine." The little ENGINATION that could.

4

Creating meaning out of the multiple systems of seemingly random and contradictory elements, echoes both the tenets of quantum physics and the traditional Jewish notion that the Torah pre-existed the world; created not *from nothing* but from the codes, matter, language, blueprint, that was always already there *en potentia*. Birthing itself into being.

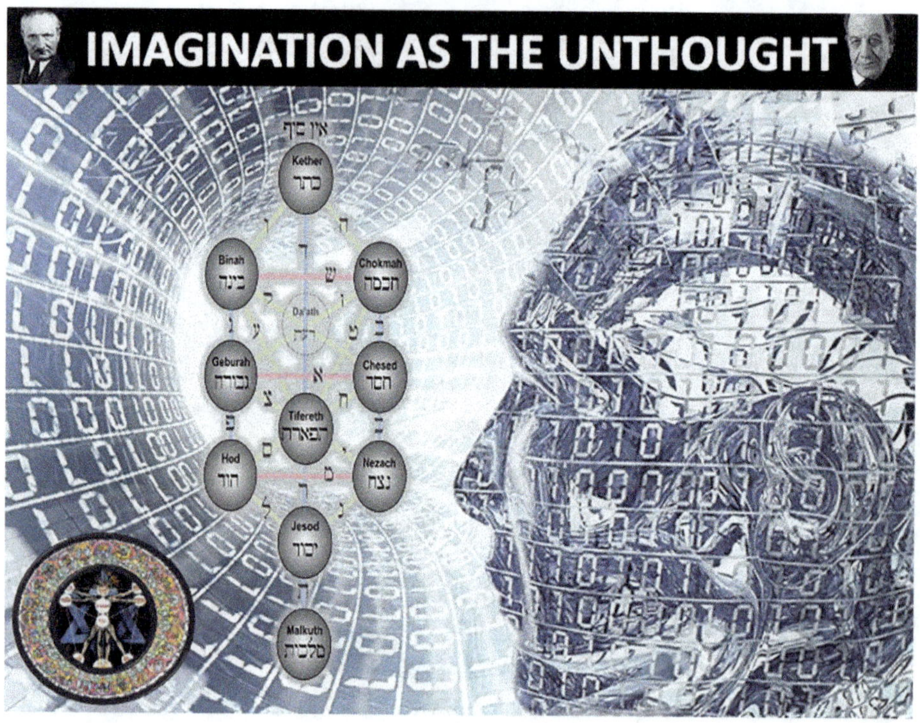

Sifting through palimpsestic constellations of logic, equations, that are already there, the imagination, a jammin'ation of riffs, drifts, grifts, like in Jazz -- or for Derrida: inspiration is never completely new but drawing on a calculus of constructs, foundations, the imagination an immersion'ation of links, subversions, excursions, perversions.

For Lacan and Zizek, the imaginary (between the symbolic and the real) *is* where identity unfolds; the site of the formation of the ego: *i-mago*. But that *i*, an amalgam analogon,[21] reminding us how the real reels in irreality, surreality, a seriality of slippery surfaces, endlessly signifying.

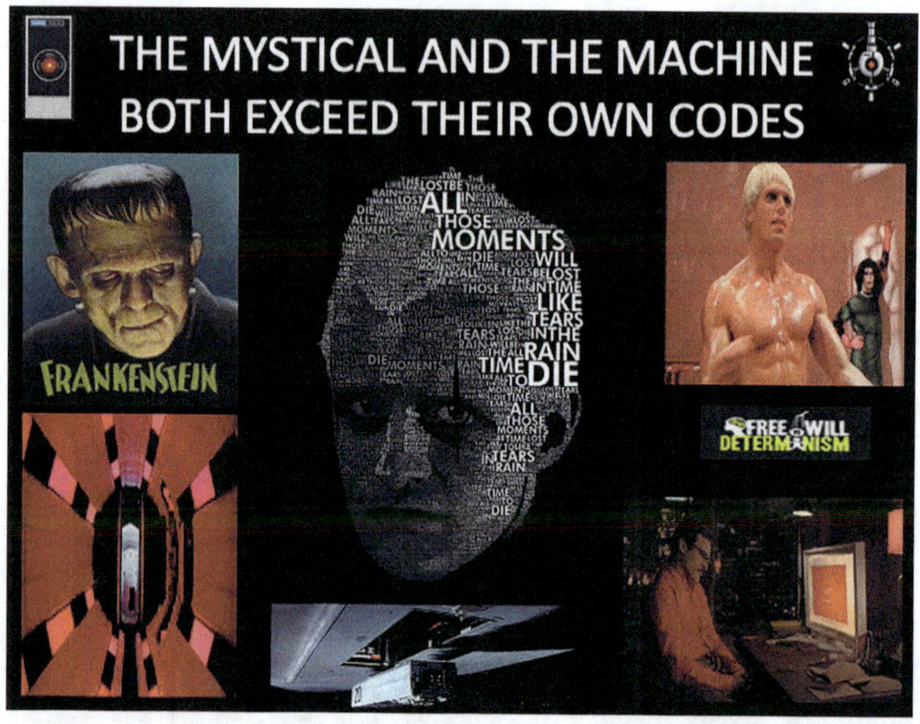

Imagination then, must be seen as an homage-ination; an homage to knowledge, perception *and* intention; navigating the conflicted nexus of lexis, deixis, parataxis; luxuriously associative and drenched in desire. In Coleridgean terms, it "fancily" secures and anchors reality. Makes the real livable --

The fancy is indeed no other than a mode of memory emancipated from the order of time and space.

(Samuel Taylor Coleridge)

And if what's fancy is what's "*so* extra," imagination then *fancily*[22] orchestrating the unthought through emotichronic / chtonic ciphers; an emojionation / all unicoded, inter-genreous and ideogrammatic; [i] mojioning us through the visceral thresholds of all that is hysterical, euphoric and full of ennui / the ever-thwarted emoticontours of representing the irrepresentable.

Or full of enWii, imagination then, a 'gameynation / the site of all possible solutions, virtually sluicing through rules codes; "a massive, multipart, global algorithm," reminding us how communication becomes a virtual matrix of language games, systems, rhythms, generating a contiguous infolding of meaning.

Imagination then, a margination; mirage'nation asking us to rethink universalized notions of nationhood --not as something totalitarian and fixed but infinitely divergent, evolving; a Baudrillardian simulacric circuit without reference or circumference, opening dialogue.

And as a merge *genre*-ation of multiple aesthetics, styles, embodying a range of difference, errance, the imagination, an invagination of communication strategies and procedures, encompassing all possible permutations and combinations; *my my my my image genre narration –*

a gemmination; or infinite redoubling, reminding us how imagination is never singular and unique but always already a memetic murmur of memories, mirrors, mires, moires, morés. In Deleuzean terms, a mirroring of duplication of reversed identification and projection always in the [play] of the double.

Because inside ima*jo*unation is *le joue*, *en jeu*; the play
of pliant pleas, a replayed display of *plaisir*. All semerotically juicy,
a magi'*joue* nation reminding us how communication is polysemous play
a superfluity of words within words, traces, affects, projections,
sliding and slipping between forces and intensities.

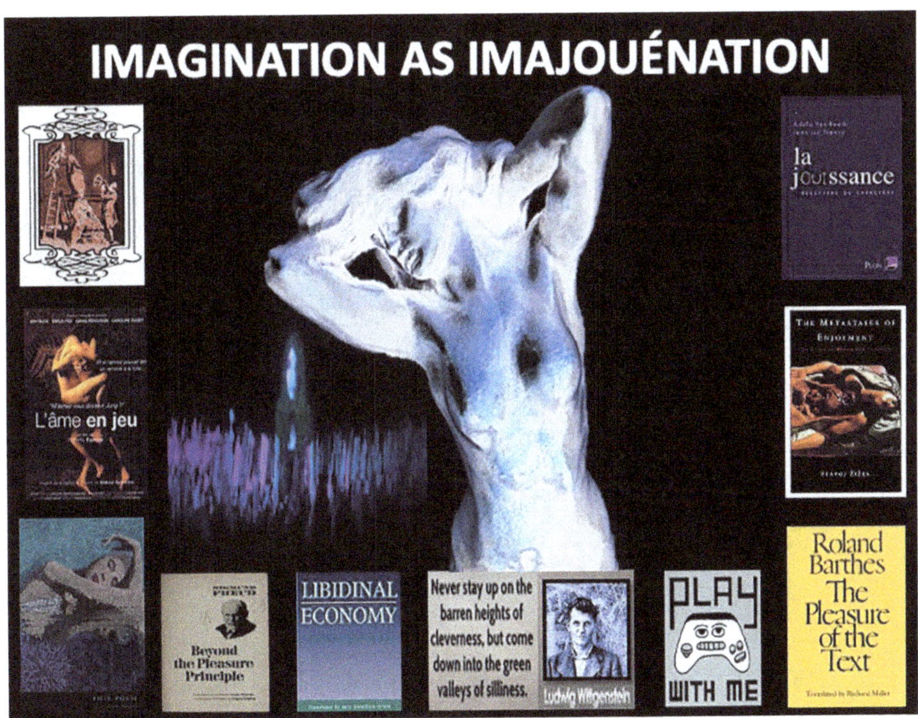

14

And thus by any stretch of the [ ] this very play, speaks to how everything is infinitely interconnected -- reverberant with our social, consumerist, communicative patterns; structures, codes, logics, idioms, a praxis of palimpsest and dissemination, generating a contiguous infolding of meaning –

Hey uh Madge you're soaking in it.
Imagine THAT!

The Ghost in the Machine
Medium, Messages and Mysticism

All media are extensions of [wo]man that cause deep and lasting changes… in [her]and transform her environment.[23]

It is in the light of magic and sorcery (potentiality, transformation, emergences), that we must rethink media as the burning projection of the consequence of gesture, voice, body image and machine and their infinite combinations[24]

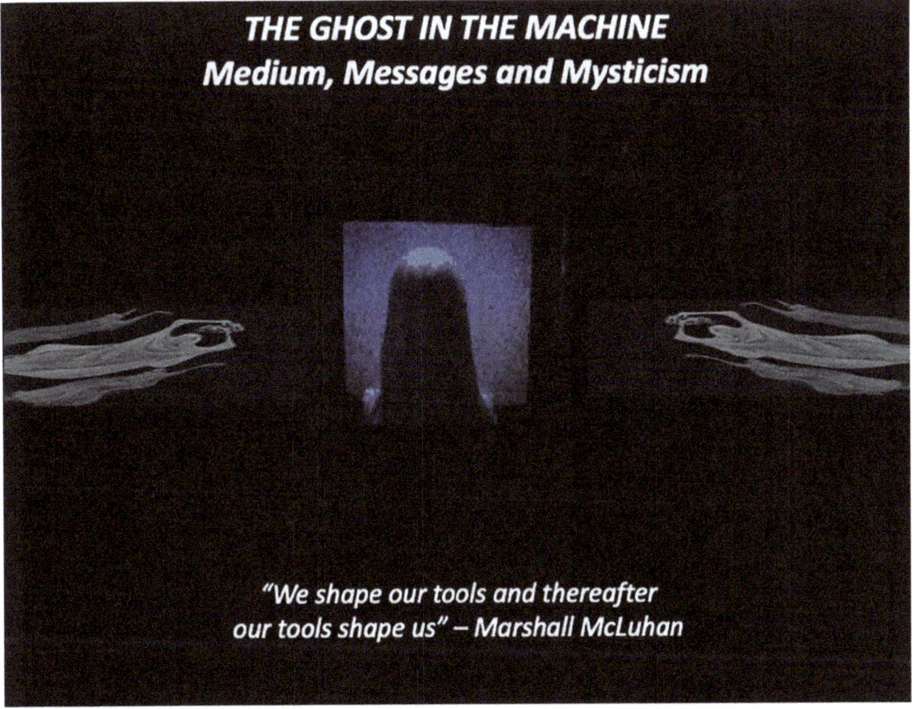

1

Historically, the Disembodied Voice referenced something mystical. A voice from the heavens. But if "mystical" refers to that which is enigmatic, obscure, logically inaccessible, beyond space and time, cyberspace is "mystical space." And if according to Derrida, "Spirit" embodies *the Same* and *Other* simultaneously, we must rethink the relationship of the mystical and the machine, not as oppositional, but that technology is eliding the binary between the physical, metaphysical, magical and the *real*, reminding us how language and thereby all knowledge is spectral, virtual, simulacric.

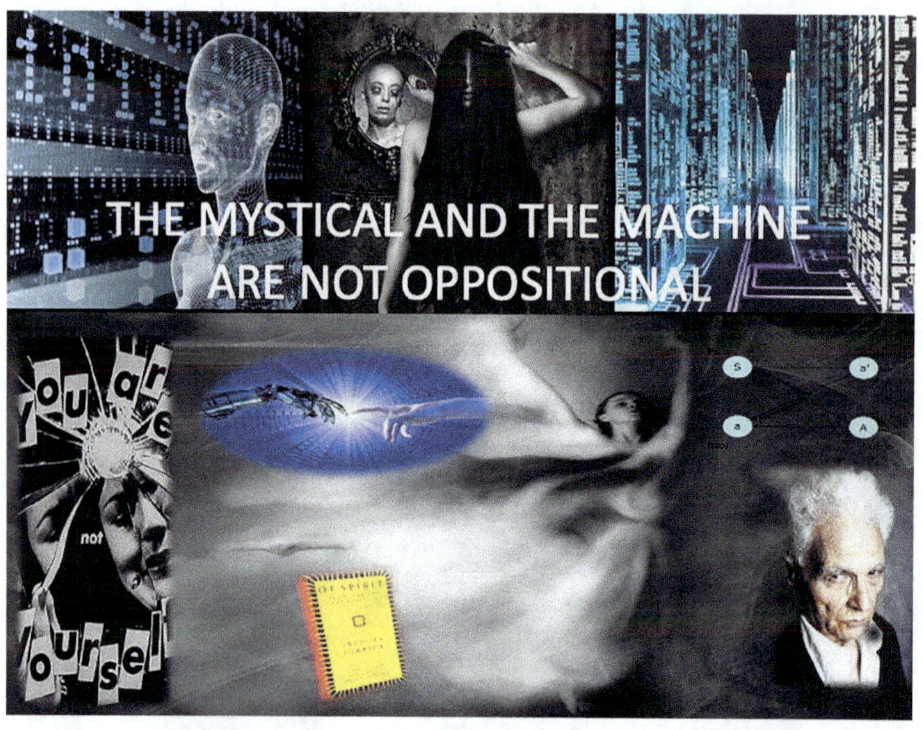

2

Throughout film history, the ghost has always lived in the machine. Whether it's the haunted internet, diabolic computers, the apparitional TV, the demonic VHS tape, amorous Replicants or the talking telephone, technology is typified as alien, other, mysterious and uncontainable; highlighted in that the word for the innerworkings of the machine, the "engine", comes from *gyn*[25], ingenious, ingénue, trickery, to engineer.

3

And as the real reels into the serial, irreal, a virtuality of invisible visibility, we are reminded how we are always *being with* specters, sliding through simulacric axes, the noumenal and the phenomenal[26] a palimpsestic contemporaneity where the real is never locatable or traceable but processual, multiplicitous and divergent. And according to Hegel, this "weaving of the spirit"[27] *is* the underground work of changing the ideological coordinates --

Accenting how both the mystical and the machine operate not physically or metaphysically but 'pataphysically -- particularly evident in that both the world[28] and the machine were created not from nothing, but from a blueprint, a series of contrapuntal codes, systems, algorithms, programs: Carrying the trace of its coding, as a resonant present, like contemporary Operating Systems impregnated with the voice of its maker, or how in the world of contemporary android development, where human minds are fully uploaded and brought to life -- are literally both beyond *and* beside themselves.

General Motors had a major role in the development of the modern Disembodied Voice through their OnStar service; cars were among the first "things" to talk to us. Manifested through media since the 60's in My Mother the Car, Killdozer, Knight Rider, Maximum Overdrive, The Car, Cars, Trucks, Wheels of Terror, or Herbie the Love Bug, foregrounding Arthur C. Clarke's famous statement, "any sufficiently advanced technology is indistinguishable from magic."[29]

Hulu darkness my old friend...

6

While in the past, the disembodied voice may have been a mechanical set of procedures (safety instructions, service protocols), or as McLuhan might say, "the servomechanism of its own extended or repeated image," perhaps true to the *ingenuity* of its *engine*, it's no longer just archiving storage but increasingly exceeding its own codes, exerting a kind of algorithmic Free Will. Reminding us that as by-products of socio gendered geo-ideological coding we are always *between* Determinism and Freedom.

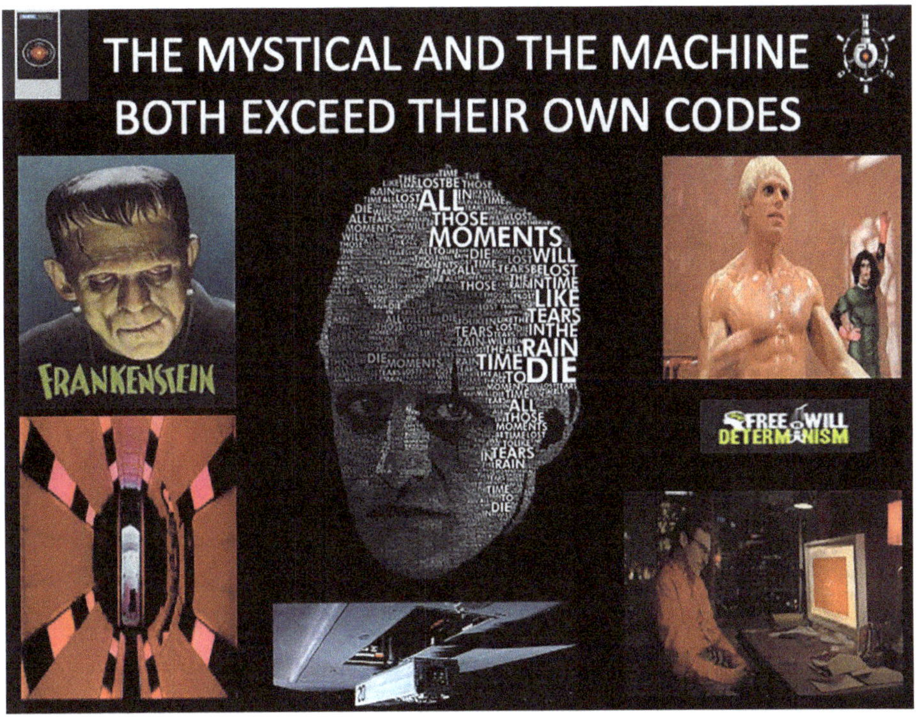

In one sense, the disembodied voice can be seen as a vestige of Julian Jayne's theory of bicameralism; which asserted that early "thought" was coming from outside itself. As late as 3000 years ago, belief was these guiding commands were issued by external 'gods'; a supernatural source. Manifested also as Original Logos, Oracular Divining, Ancestral Worship.

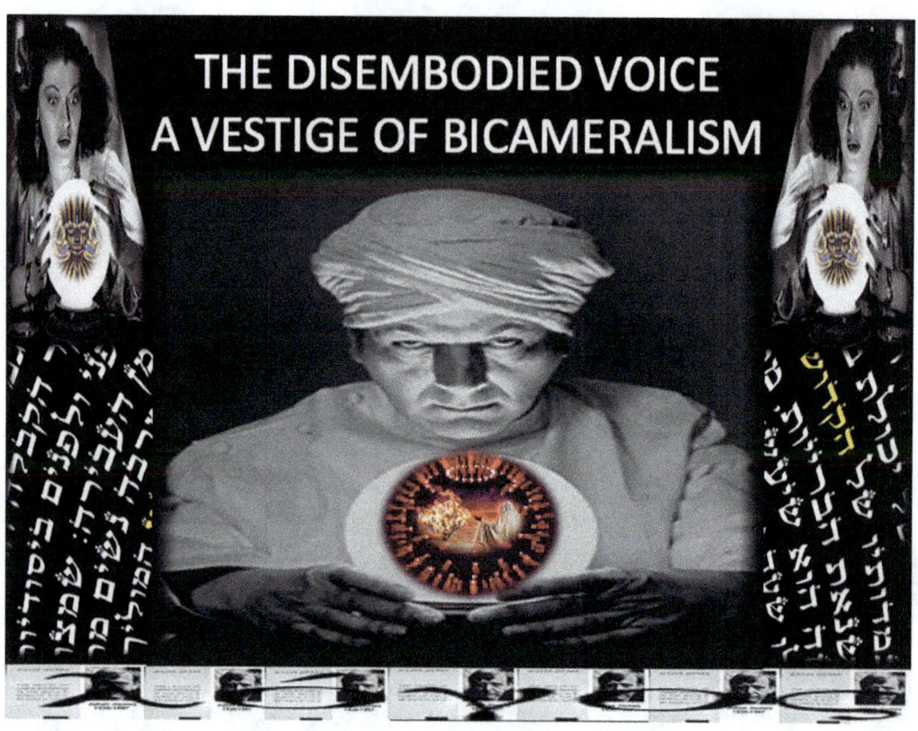

Similarly, according to Walter Ong, "thought" was understood as a kind of outside coding: anthropomorphic voices, an exteriorization of an internal state which becomes interiorized. And as thought becomes talk becomes voice, the "still small voice" echoes and deflects, reflects the voice as a resourced sourcery of "flickering signifiers."

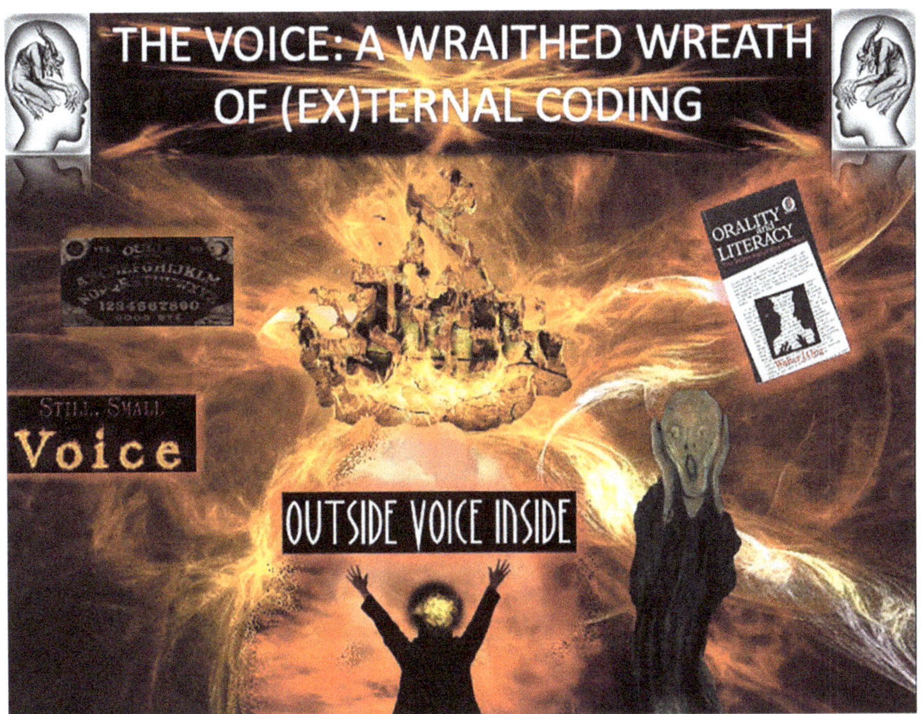

Upton Sinclair's *Mental Radio* points to how the Voice's telepathy[30] is related to the telegraph; how in the 1800's, Spiritualism erupted from the telegraph,[31] telephone, radio. Oracular and ancestral, apostrophic and apparitional -- *Voici! Voila! viva voce* Google Voice, Voice Finger, Voice Typing: media reminds us how voice vociferous and viscous, veils, unveils, avails in vaporous verity.

10

For Walter Benjamin, "voice" becomes a simulation of auratic[32] effects. For Cixous and Derrida, it hovers as a ghostly trace, echo specter; an excess of an excess, all lexi-nomadic and elec*trace*cally charged, highlighting how the machine *is* the voice of the voice misc-en screaming in the polyglossic intertextual miasma.

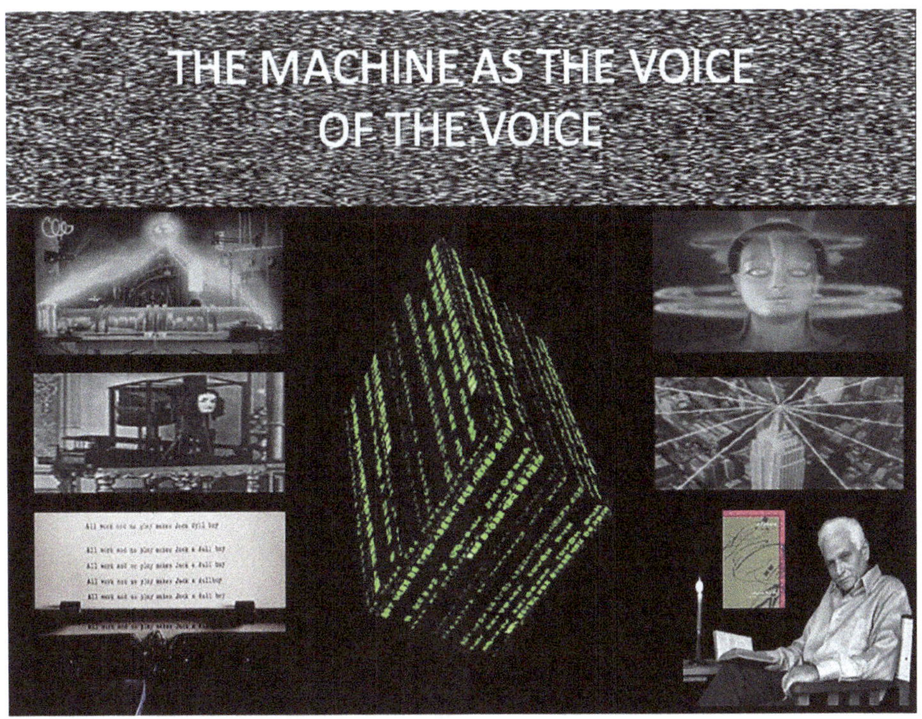

With the development of algorithmic personalities, Disembodied Voices started to become more human. Apple's, Siri, referencing Circe's Sirens suckin' sailors into the sea, "understands what you say, knows what you mean." Whether its Siri, Alexa, Echo, Nest, Dot, Cortana, Cleverbot, contemporary AI reminds us how the medium IS the message, massaging your *sans* and your sensorium.

12

Increasingly personalized, this technology is taking McLuhan's, "Extensions of Man" to a radical place; not just as a personalization of our media, but as an intensification, amplification, causing deep and lasting changes, transform[ing] our environment. Now not only an Instagrammatic döppleGANGer of scrolling selfies, but as exposed in her 2019, "Can I Touch It," with the aid of cutting edge laboratories in Japan and the US, Whitney Cummings has a sex Robot cloned of herself, exposing how through detailed customization of both physical (height, weight, face, voice, skin tone, breast size, nipple shape and genitalia) and personality traits (intelligence and emotional range), not only is a ghost, a host inside the machine but how it raises questions of sentience, dissensions, tensions in the extensions of [wo]man.[33]

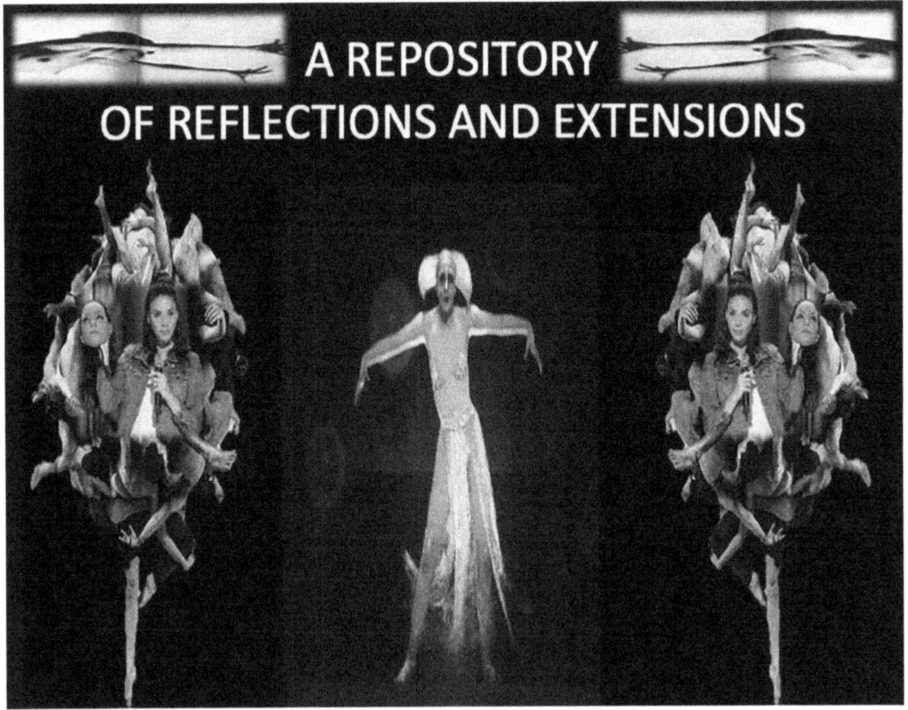

This hyper-personalization of the "Other" not only reminds us how the Self and Other are not dichotomous but an infinite mirroring of effects, and *a la* Symbolic Interactionism,[34] constructed *in relation* to each other. This is uncannily similar to the ancient Kabbalistic practice of creating a Golem:[35] Through a series of codes, combinations and lexical distribution, early rabbis created a "companion" *in their own image.*

Like the OS of Spike Jonez', *Her* or contemporary "living" avatars formed in the image of their maker(s), Golems were not just an example of mastering the code but were created to serve their creator.[36] Some performed simple tasks like drawing water from a well or protected villages from attack. In the medieval period, Rabbi Samuel, father of Judah the Pious, was said to have had a golem as his valet. In the 16th Century, Rabbi Elija of Chelm created his as a servant, and Rabbi Yehuda Loew, the Marharal of Prague, used his golem (which he named) Yosele to protect the Jews of his community.

15

According to Dag Kittlaus, *the maker of Siri,* "we were trying to build the world's first true virtual personal assistant…Siri was built to get things done."[37] And thus, urging us to re-see the body not as increasingly unnecessary, but as in Harraway's, *A Cyborg Manifesto,*[38] how "the machine is us, our process, an aspect of our embodiment"; and evokes a "kinetic body" that both generates and obscures signification.

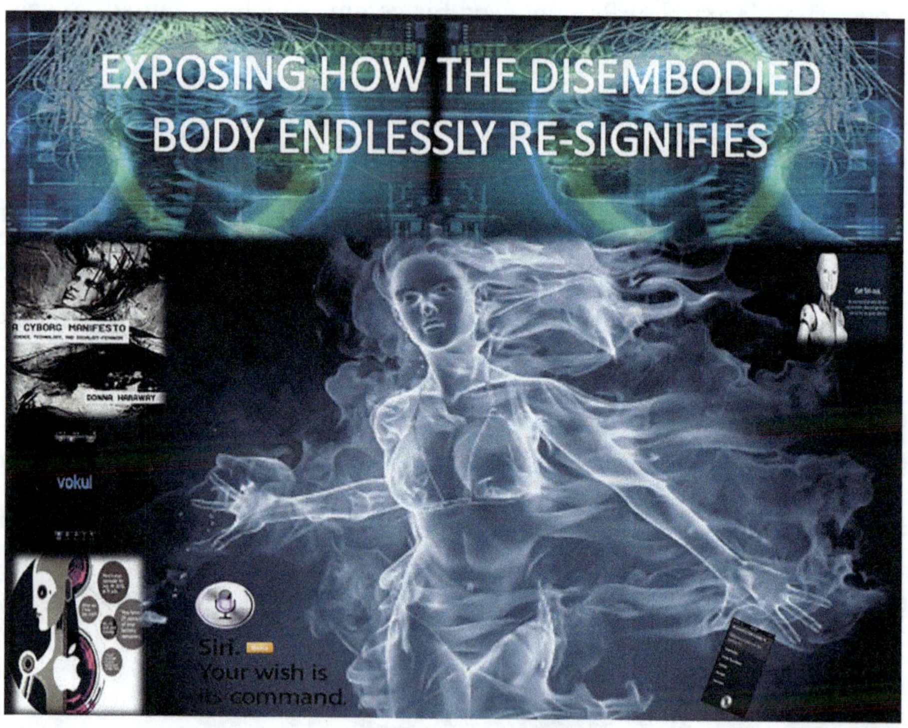

Similarly, for Johanna Drucker[26] "the visual form of the letter on the screen [is] fully material... even though the 'letter' exists as a stored sequence of binary digits with no tactile, material apparency to it." Or for both Artaud and Deleuze and Guattari's, "body without organs,"[39] an immaterial body which enacts the Lacanian or Zizekian notion of desire; schizophrenetically inaccessible, in process and ultimately out of reach.[40]

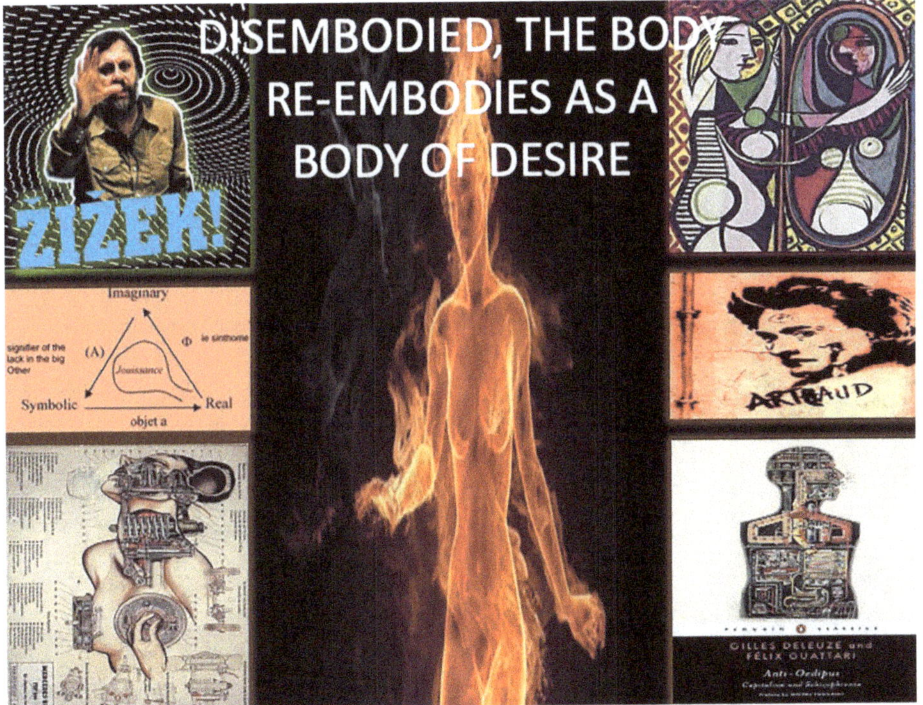

Or in the case of Aura Dolls, North America's first *Sex Doll Brothel*, the body *is* in reach. Located just outside of Toronto, Canada, the establishment "allows customers to anonymously pay for sexual services with high tech, silicone dolls," and promises to give clients a "realistic sensual experience with a girl who is made just for you." Servicing its clientele with "the world's most beautiful silicone ladies", where one can choose from six "life-like" dolls, each with its own online profile complete with a name, photos, and brief bio, between the horro' and the "aura," the signoras of Aura not only are erotic replicants in the age of mechanical reproduction, but enact the ironic literality of how (in the words of Walter Benjamin) –

"The beautiful "character" unfolds. All of those present become comically iridescent. At the same time one is pervaded by their aura."[41]

And thus, in the "illuminosity" of "transitional materialities," through all that is animate, inanimate, defleshistic and fetishized, between the voice and the body, where the *body proper is* improper impropriotous riotous, raging in a scrolling corollary of radical mutability, (extensions of extensions), we inhabit not a taunting ontology but *hauntology --*

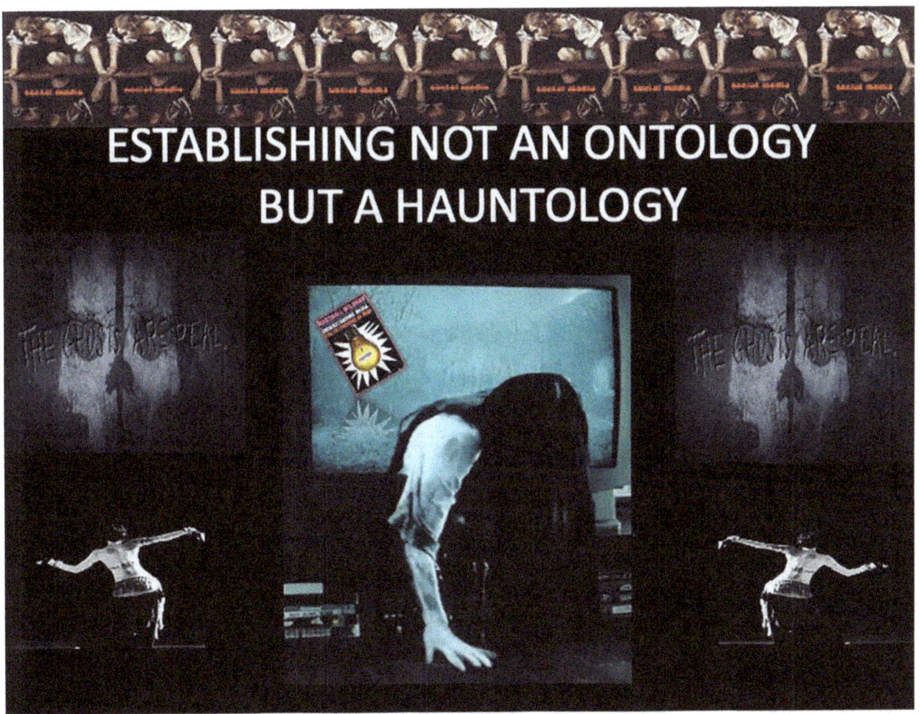

where **the ghost *IS* the machine**, binding time through and across symbols that assemble resemble, re-assemble in a shifting ensemble. All spaced out and palimpsestic, as we move backwards into the future, with virtual companions (now, with not only algorithmic decision-making programming, but with the ability to retain memory, and learn),[42] with intelligence, emotion and volition, increasingly, "our tools are shaping us."

And as in McLuhan's *narcissus narcosa*,[43] we must wake up.

Medium in a Messy Age
Communication in the Era of Technology
or
The Media Ecology of Conceptual Poetry

1

Marshall McLuhan, re-citing Ezra Pound[44] claims "[poets] are the antennae of the race." And as radar, acts as 'an early alarm or warning system'[45] enabling us to discover social and political targets in time to cope with and learn from them. Thus, it is the POETS that have the utmost relevance not only to communication and media study but to the development of media controls.

McLuhan writes of using avant-garde poetics, "to organize the data of the historian and the social scientist," recognizing the value of reading the records and statistics of technology through cultural forms.[46] 50 yrs later, Conceptual Poetry[47] arrives, and operates by obsessively archiving and cataloguing cultural spam; not creating, but "managing" information.

According to Friedrich Kittler, "the new sciences and technologies made it necessary for [poets] to renounce the imagination."[48] Conceptual Poetry, self-described as "uncreative writing" uses word processing, databasing, sampling, coding, cutting pasting and mashing up[49] unloved language, the debased language of media & advertising; focusing more on the initial concept than the final product.

Just as the telegraph turned words into a commodity, Rob Fitterman's pop-up "Word Shop"[50] selling language, creates an "information economy"[51] highlighting how language is both material object and act of transference; media, message, content and container [52] in an endless re-marketability of production, consumption, transcription and trans*action*.

Like how Pound saw literature as "news that STAYS news,"[53] imparting crucial information about meaning-making as it circulates through culture, McLuhan saw the newspaper as a mosaic, (where "the dateline replaced the storyline"); an intertextual matrix of extracted maculates, bracketed tracts, hacked fractures, where you can read it in any order you want.

6

Throughout history, Conceptual Poets have used the newspaper as source material for their investigations into differing models of communication: Marinetti, Mallarmé, the Italian Futurists,[54] Wyndham Lewis, Picasso and the Cubists, Tzara, Schwitters, Gysin, Burroughs; all beaten bruised *BLAST*ed and cut-up re-sourcing systems of semiotic slippage.

A poignant manifestation of this is Goldsmith's *Day*, a word-for-word transcription of the entire New York Times newspaper for September 1, 2000.[55] By making no distinction between article, editorial and ads, disregarding all typographical treatments, *Day* not only questions the hierarchy of information but foregrounds the diversity of communication models comprised of "yesterday's news."

8

This sense of re-creating the past through mimicry and transcription inevitably results in a re-valuation of history. For Zizek, "to build a future one has to ransack the past," McLuhan's "rearview mirror," Benjamin's "Angel of History"[56] ceaselessly waft into the future, where contents regenerate in an autopoieic past of a past of re-passed postulates.

And in a repast of a past, poised, parsed and repurposed, drawing from the miasma of our cultural intellectual archive, "Lingual Ladies,"[57] my 2013 parody of Beyoncé's hit "Single Ladies," functions as a culturally translated ideological mash-up. Featuring cameos from the texts or likeness of Gertrude Stein, Ludwig Wittgenstein, the Italian and Russian Futurists, Karl Marx, Jacques Derrida, Emmanuel Levinas, Walter Benjamin, bpNichol, Baruch Spinoza, Hélène Cixous and Hannah Arendt (all floating through the boppy mistranslation of a pop song), it not only de-hierarchizes the distinction between "high art" elitist discourse and the "lowbrow" seeming banality of mass media -- but if a meme, a unit of cultural information virally replicating itself through language -- it acts as a kind of rallying cry for the women of Conceptual Poetry to "put their pens up," engage in a vital act of cultural translation: "make a text of radical memes."

10

Conceptual Poetry as a hybridized medium, not only reframes history, but Law, Biology and Digital Technologies. Taking Burrough's,[58] "language is a virus" literally, Christian Bök's *Xenotext Experiment* implants bacteria into DNA and shoots it into space, attempting to engineer a life-form so that it will not only store a poem, but becomes a writing machine.[59]

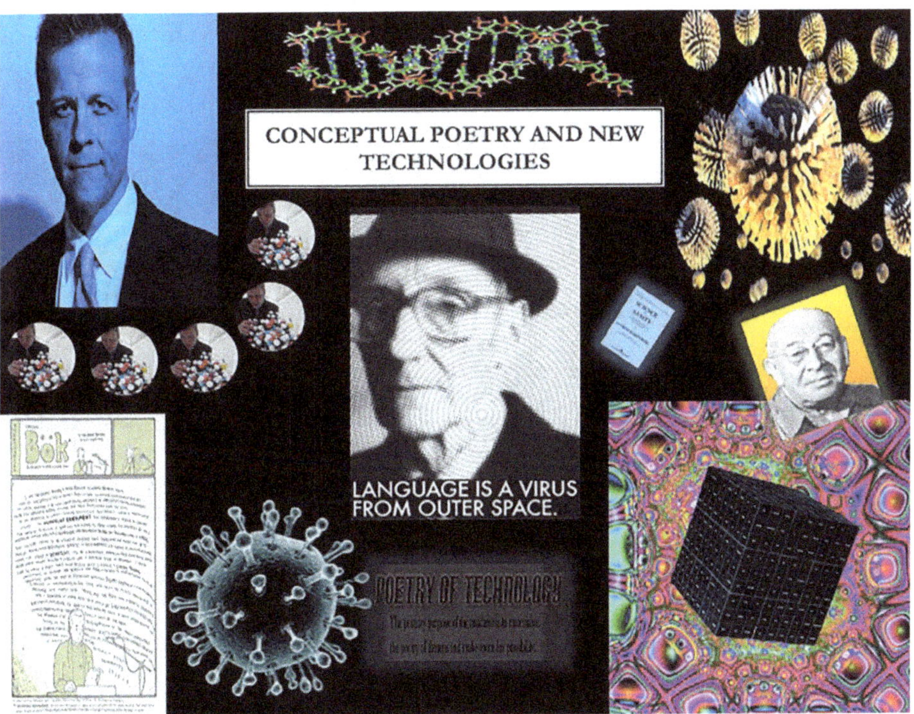

The Spectaular Vernacular

Not only is Conceptual Poetry questioning genre, but the hierarchic domains of discourse. Urging us to look at the poetic qualities of the excluded languages of the "everyday": The internet, the street, graffiti, radio broadcasts and news reports. On December 8, 2014, filmed live and globally broadcast, Kenneth Goldsmith read at the White House -- a listing of traffic reports from *1010 WINNS*, as poetry.

12

And we are still gonna have to get through, uh, a pretty bad rush hour. Already we've got major delays on, uh, Seventh and Eighth Avenue as you, uh, make your way through the Midtown area. Seventh Avenue delays begin right out of Central Park, all the way down through Times Square. Broadway's impacted obviously, Ninth and Tenth Avenues seeing more traffic as well, but not as bad as, uh, heading through the Times Square area. Meanwhile, on the East Side it's a torture test, because a lot of the, uh, side streets are taking a beating, especially through the 40's and 50's. That will impact traffic at the 59th Street Bridge, which is jammed coming into Manhattan. Right now you've also got jam-ups on the Brooklyn Bridge, bumper-to-bumper to Brooklyn but the lower roadway is wide open. The Brooklyn Bridge is swamped. The FDR Drive's not looking very good either, bumper-to-bumper right off the Manhattan Bridge. Meanwhile the West Side delays begin in the 70's and they go south all the way to the Battery Tunnel[60]

<h1 style="text-align:center">13</h1>

In the diction of the "ordinary"[61] and "everyday," *Traffic* then becomes a kind of probe,[62] a web of disparate ideas, altering perception, working associatively, full of rupture, rapture, scripturous apertures. Operating as an aphoristic machine of punning and metonymy, auxiliary lanes and interchanges; weaves, yields, swerves out from its own gridlock.

Further investigations into dyssemic ecologies are ever-present with Conceptual Poetry's cousin Flarf; whose mandate is to create poems out of Google Search results. Whether reworking Shakespearean sonnets into rogaine bunnies, Pokemon Peanuts or Peppermint Jihad, within the anonymized algorhythms of reshuffled junkspeech, poems become a virtual chatroom.

Canadian poets, bissett, and Beaulieu also offer probing investigations into meaning production as an interlingual ecosystem enacting what Guattari might call a *"transversal practice"* of surfaces with "a-signifying semiological dimensions" that establish figural narratives where the figure, refigured in a continually shifting ground.

Not only calling attention to the materiality of language, but the process of reading is the focus of Craig Dworkin's *Parse*. A translation of Abbott's 1874 guide, *How to Parser*,[63] sentences are converted into descriptions of their own grammatical structure. In parsed plays *pursed* with replaced plosives, *Parse* parracidically performs and exposes language's impossible transparency.

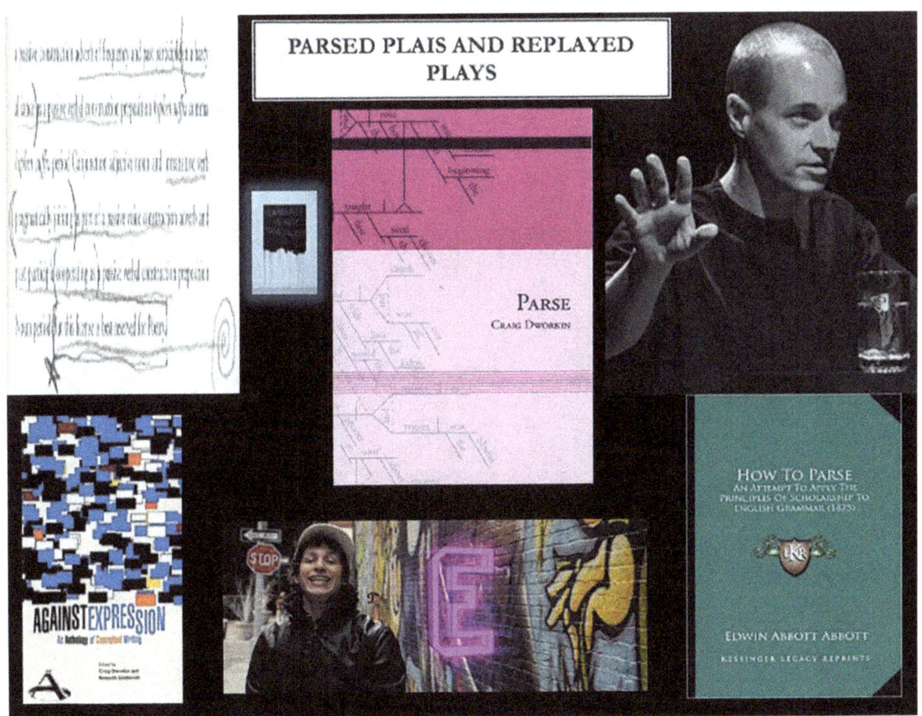

Thus, for Conceptual Poets, the poem is not just a repository of information but reframing, repurposing, recreating not so much in "The Age of Mechanical Reproducibility, but in the age of mimetic proliferation. Exposing itself as units of cultural knowledge virally replicating itself, it's doing with language what language has always done for itself, resembling something it is not[64].

18

As a container of a container of kinships, contours, re-*connaître*,[65] kinesis, Conceptual Poetry reminds us, how in the age of digital media, (as language is poured into ads, docs, databased, morphed, animated spammed and spit out), it *is* the environment for developing new and methodological tools for investigating the material and the circulatory aspects of communication.[66]

Refracted Facts

The Crazy Talk of *Checking In*
A Postmanic *'Pata* Semantics

In conversation with (and re-iterating what Terry Moran said in his 2017 Alfred Korzybski Memorial Lecture), "if politicians knew more about poetry, the world would be a better place."

So, between the profound and the confound, meddling in the muddled middle of re-modelled sanity,

"she talk crazy talk"
(Chillawack)

1

According to Neil Postman, "stupid talk" is talk that is ineffective, confused, decontextualized and distorted; talk that does not or cannot achieve its purposes. "Crazy talk" however, though effective is unreasonable, irrational; requires that we be mystified, suspend critical judgment, accept premises without question, and (frequently) abandon entirely the idea that language ought to be connected with reality.[67] The problem of crazy talk, is not in what it does *for* you but in what it does *to* you.

2

Poetry, however, offers an escape from this dichotomy; a way of entering language structures, powers and foundations that can lead to inquiry and action. According to poet/theorist, Norman Fischer, poems "don't [] *transmit* meaning but muddle up meaning." Though meaning to mean, words never mean what they say or say what they mean but present an impossible aporia of porous rapport.

3

And though for Postman, anything other than *clear* is "stupid" or "crazy," for Fischer (and Canadian poet, painter and sound artist, bill bissett), meaning is a kind of tyranny. And, as the text tempts, tremors, terrorizes, teases, torments and titillates, we must learn how to loosen our grip. As Jack Kerouac might say, embrace its "ripple." In the words of Prince,

"Let's Go Crazy."

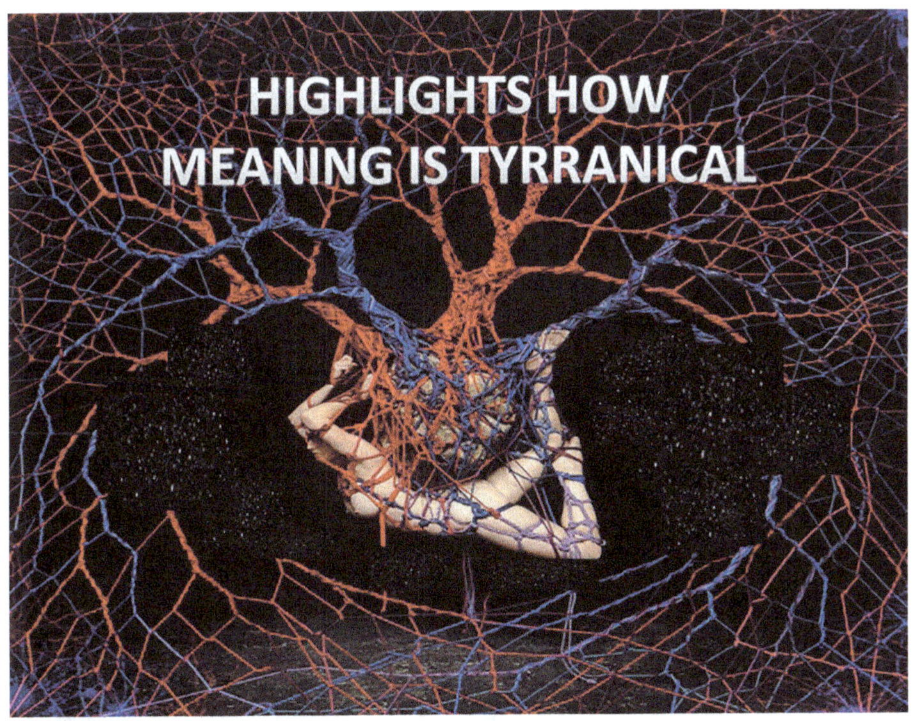

Forging a site of radical grafting of "crazy talk" linkages and ludic identities, *Checking in* my 2018 book, drawing from ever-shifting, contrapuntal semantic environments, is composed of a listing of faux facebook updates and speaks to the ongoing desire for truth and clarity while acknowledging how fraught with myth and slippage that is. Like how Korzybski's non-Aristotelian research draws upon relativity theory, quantum mechanics and mathematical logic, embracing the differences between symbols and reality (words and references), it plays with ways we just "can't *handle* the truth."

Through a satiric tour through the shards and fragments of literary and post-consumerist culture, it creates a kind of algorhythmic rhapsody, reminding us how the internet is not only voyeuristic but it's data, a mirage, and as such, speaks to the way we seek answers, but (in 'pataphysical terms) answers to questions that have never been asked. We seek fulfillment but enter an unsettling, uninhibited flow of information where every data point only refers back to itself and the culture of techno-capitalism of the web.

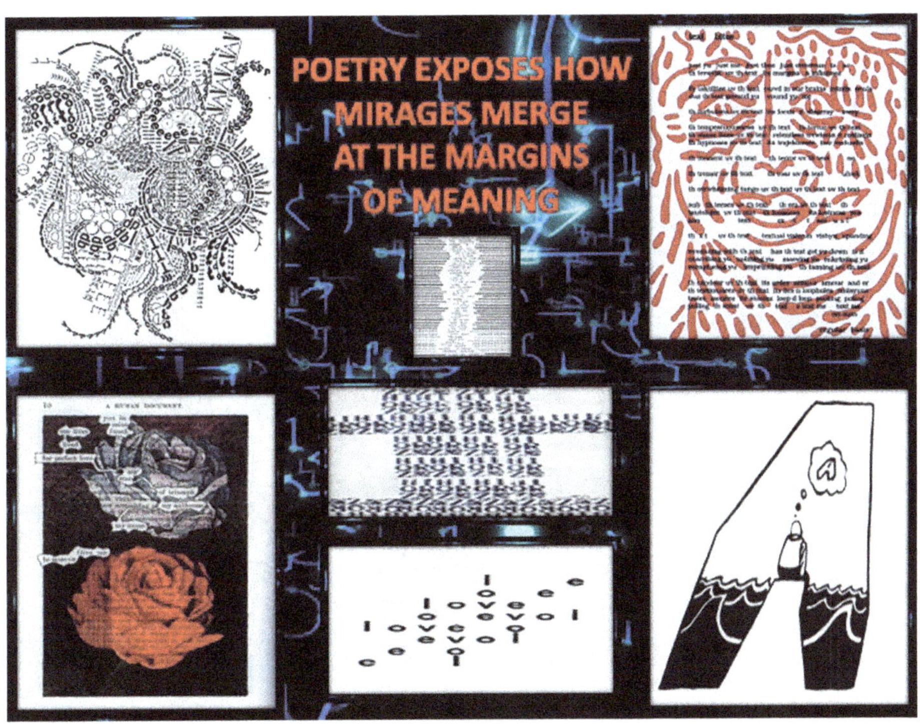

Truth becomes a negotiation of ever-shifting values, assumptions, collaging past present and future. In Zizekian terms, "Truth [can never be] enforced because the moment fidelity to Truth functions as an excess enforcement, we are no longer dealing with a Truth, [but] with fidelity to a Truth Event";[68] thus, what's presented as true, (as Lance Strate might say, "effects of effects of effects of effects"), a complex flex of conflictual facts; refracted acts enacted through multiple Postmanic semantic environments.

For Baudrillard, the discourse of truth is ever-elusive and everything scoffs at its own truth seduction. And though we are driven by an obscene rage to uncover the sercret of *s'écrits*; to arrive at "the naked truth," which haunts all discourse, this furious search is both a "crazy" and "stupid nostalgia both *for* and *of* the infinite.

Or read through Derrida, "truth," is always already a representation. All language is rhetorical rather than denotative and any emphatic statement carries within it a cultural, lexical and political history that reinforces, engenders, instigates, propagates a metaphysics of presence, (ie the Husserlian "now"). And thus, it's crucial to continually contextualize, uncover the fabrication, analyze the violence that this initiates and sustains; seek out the hidden assumptions and reveal the inherent violence of this dichotomy, and not lose sight of the larger systems of subordination.

Acknowledging this spectral fluidity, Jews, at *Rosh HaShana*, blow the shofar, a ram's horn (as a kind of wake-up call). ***TERUAH!!*** In both Hebrew and Aramic, TERUAH, homiletically comes from "[t]ra'ah" which means shaky. Thus, translinguistically, from the beginning of the world, what is [true] is re-routed as volatile and uncertain; destabilized flecks of facts in flux.

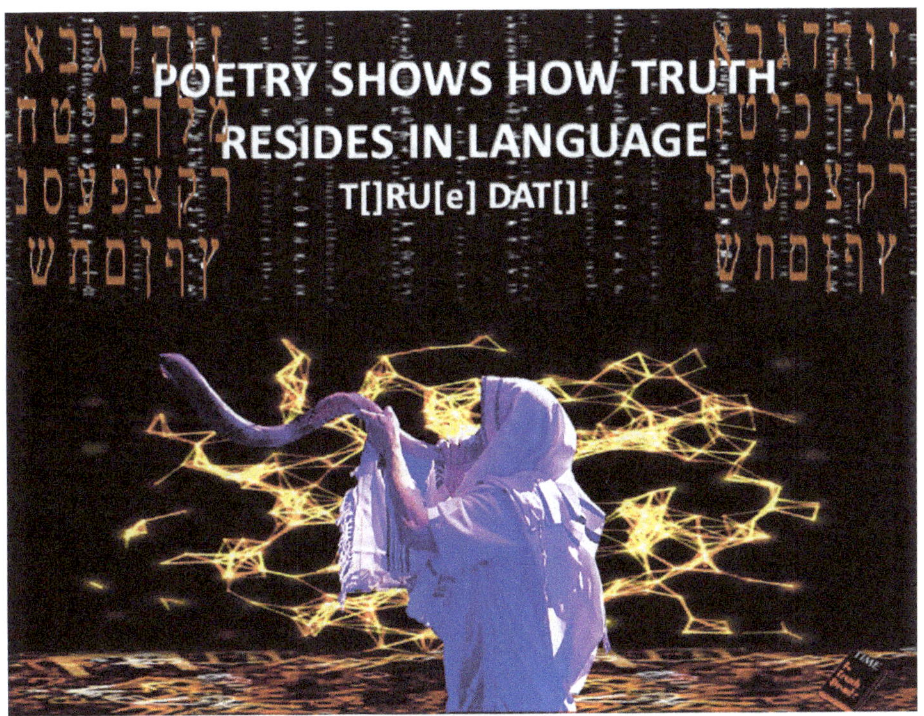

Using Baudrillard as a guide, we are reminded that it's through our pop culture, screens, books; repeatability masking, mirroring and fragmentation, that truth is always already (as both Borges and Jabès might also say), a point in space that contains all other points. Anyone who gazes into it can see everything in the universe from every angle simultaneously, a re-imaged confluence of masques and distortions, or in Joycean terms, *"a commodius vicus of recirculation,"* that both covets and foregrounds its caveats.

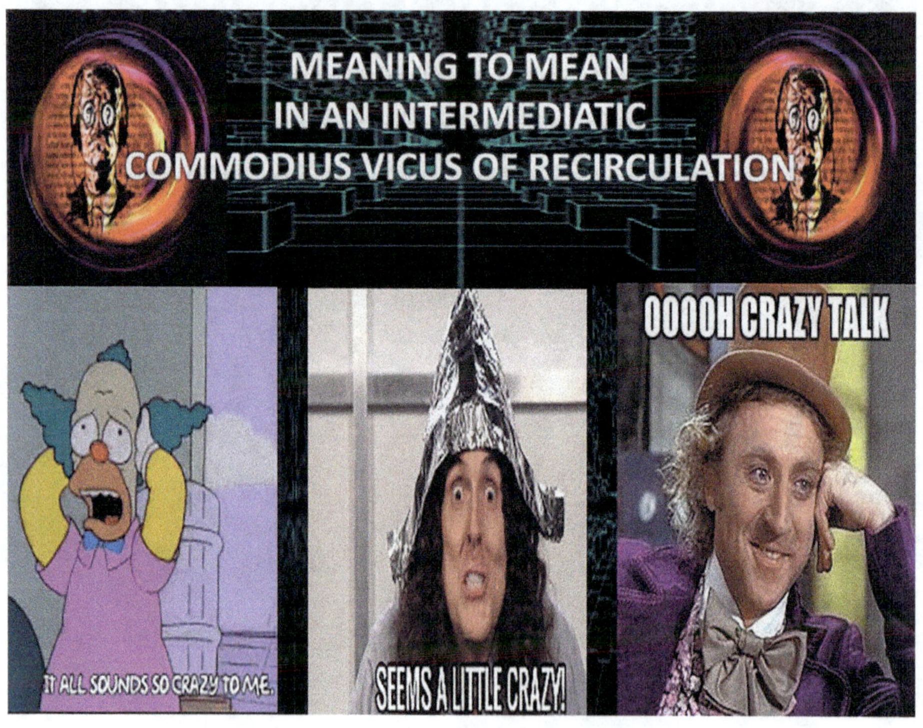

11

CHECKING IN[69]

Jules Verne is listening to the Dark Side of the Moon
Ziggy Stardust is playing Space Invaders
The Wind-Up Bird is Dreaming of Electric Sheep
Papa Smurf is in the House of Mirth
Neil Postman always rings twice
Marie Antoinette disabled her cookies / but is eating cake
Decartes is before the Horse
Nobodaddy is Putting Baby in the Corner
Nude is descending a Staircase to Heaven
Fancy Bread is in the Heart and in Thy head / and also at Balthazars
Sisyphus is at the Hard Rock®
Marshall McLuhan is getting his Medium massaged
Blondie is Asking you to Call her
Yahoo! Is opening some Happy Tabs
Hansel and Gretl are getting baked
Icarus is flying high
Moses is smashing his Tablet
UBER Allis is driving a Cab
Alfred Korzybski is using Wayz

In conclusion, perhaps an antidote for "crazy talk" is to borrow from both poetic and media ecological thinking, acknowledging that meaning does not just rest in specific semantic environments, but mired in cycles of seduction and elision, d/elusion, illusion, perhaps better our search be not for resolution but a re-sluicion, resisting outmoded tropes of truth, closure and clarity, and revel instead in the visceral swirls, lexical textures, fictions, friction, fracas and fragments -- where what's "true" is a teleological roux, and the "real" is always already re-produced; a resonant present re-presented / porous, possible and prescient.

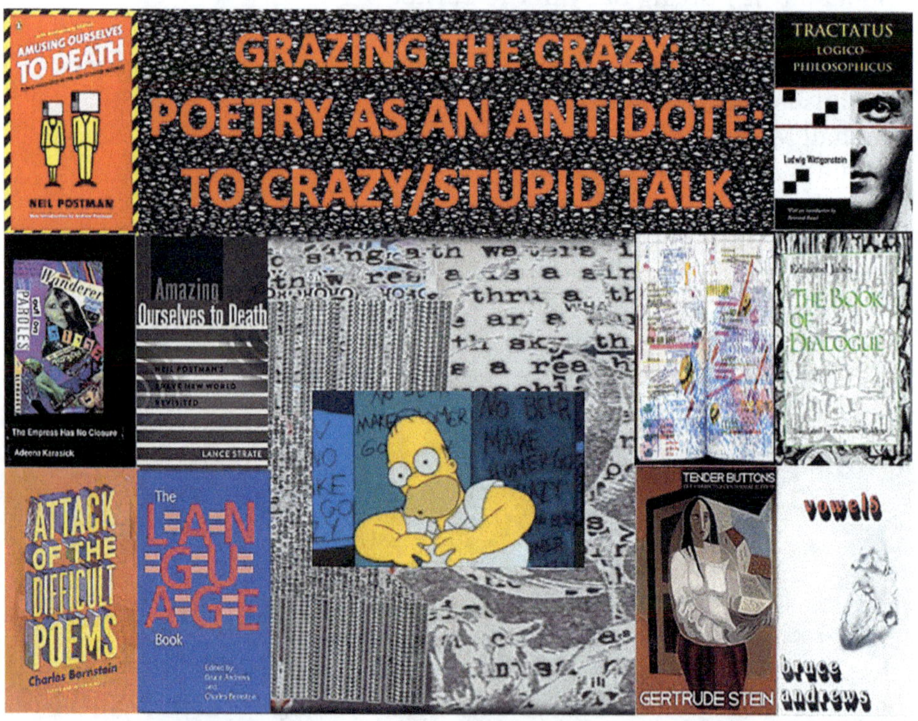

Maps and Terrortories,
PreScience and In-Sanity
bill bissett and the Non-Allness of Abstraction

or

Chants Rants Rattles and Trance
bill bissett and the KaBABEListics
of Acoustic Space

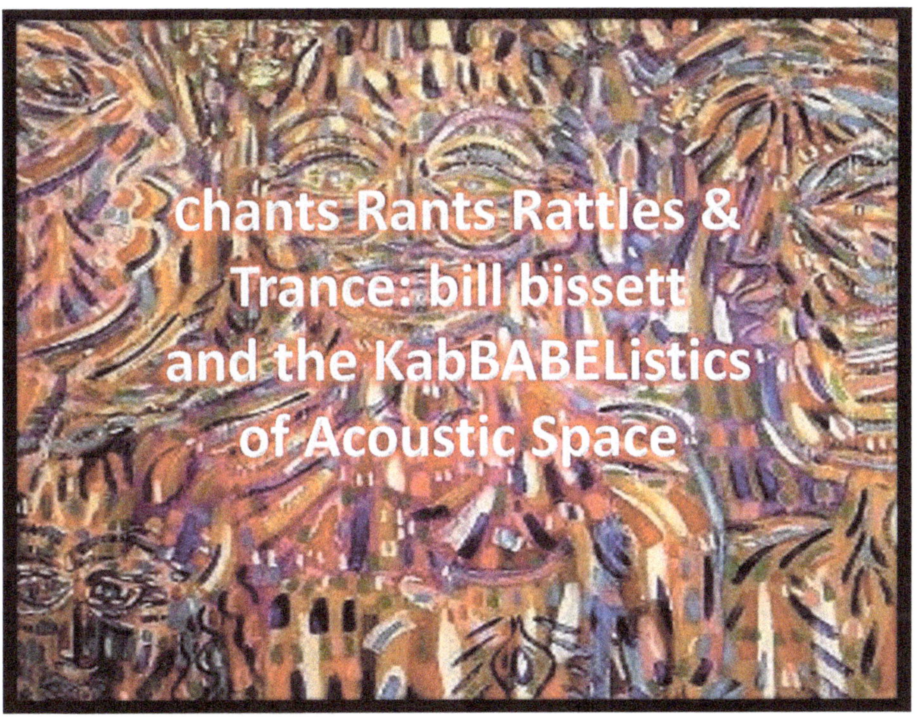

1

Between the map and the territory; between Britain and America, structures of power and subversion; embodying a range of de-colonized identities; as painter, performer, film critic,[70] shaman, concrete, sound, language and lyrical poet straddling a Dutch American, Canadian, French, Scotch and "lunarian" heritage; between *science* and *sanity*, bill bissett inscribes a language of textual hybridity which "xplodes" into an intra-subjective matrix of differential locations, allocations, r/elations, inscribing a Kozybskian model of non-elementalism.

2

And perhaps like how for Marshall McLuhan, acoustic space,
the "inner landscape of poetry, is a field of discontinuous components,"
fields of relation, elation, erration, dynamic and in flux,
creating its own dimensions *out of itself*
within these sonoric axes of fracturous raptures --

3

we are reminded of Korzybski's axiom that "structure
[is always] a complex of relations," [71] resounding
with not so much an efficient, but a coefficient causality
where effect begets effect in an erratic praxis of secular vectors,
a synnexes of lexis, heuristic excess, a nexus of affect,
celebrating all that is unclean, *in sani*

and as such, enter an "asylum," where language is both a haven *and* a schizophonophelia, full of abstraction and "logical insanity." And through a chanting insistence, we enter Eliot's auditory imagination, penetrate layers of the unconscious, exploding not just into an aural landscape but a languescape, a sonorific matrix of wor[l]ds, levels, layers of being created out of syllabic axioms –

and in-so-doing, (as McCaffery might say), undermines capitalism's agenda in how it exceeds standard models of exchange.[72]

For this disorientation effects alternate states of being, disrupts normative thought patterns –

and erupts in a kind of combinatorial erogenous deviance; a vibrational political sonocentrics of rhythm, pulse, plaise, plays, liaised, laced with "narrative enigma," "oral aisles" of exits, entrances / en trances

highlighting language's transformational capacities,
foregrounding its corporeal and material affects, how it stimulates,
engages the nervous system, establishing a vibratory nexus
transmitting intelligence and emotion simultaneously.

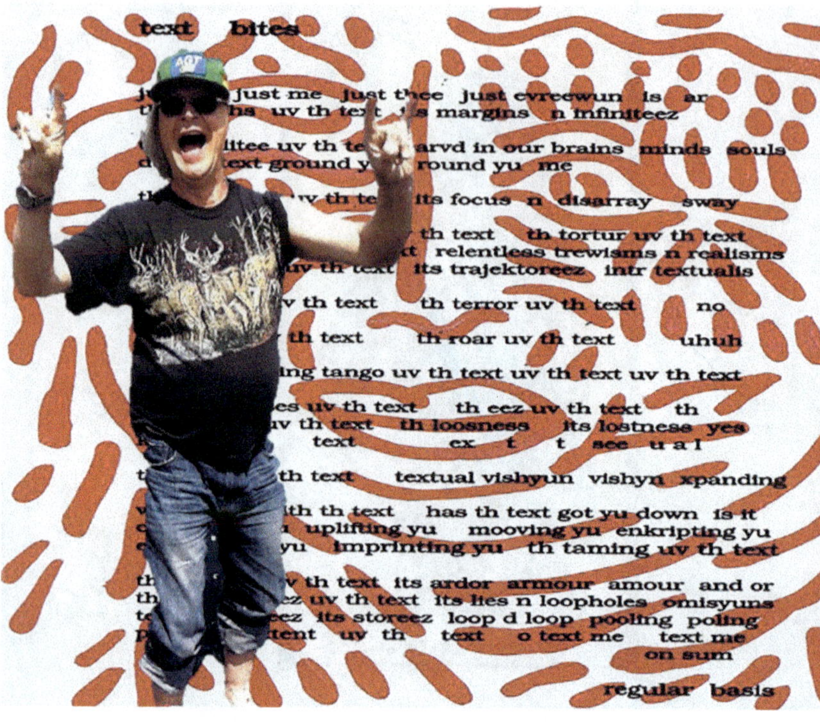

And, if according to bissett, "here is a here is a here" as "a is an art is an artery," we are reminded how IS is never what it is; that á la Saussure and Derrida, language is always pointing to that which it is not. Not just echoing the Korzybskian theorem or Gertrude Stein's, no [ ]here [ ]here, but highlights also how according to 13th C. Kabbalists,[73] it is through the chanting of the letters that life is brought into existence; and through letter combination and permutation, the world is remade anew.

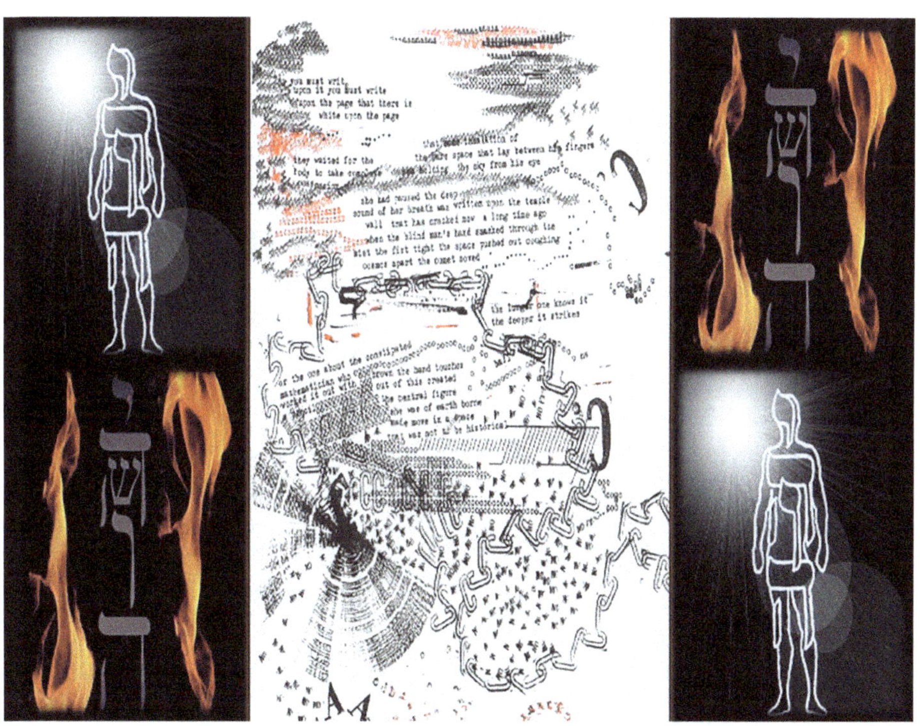

And through this renegotiation of sound and texture,
bissett is not only reminding us of the relationship between language and reality;
but is *also* uncannily mirroring the Kabbalistic practice of creating a Golem.

As outlined by Rabbi Eliezar Rokeach of Worms,[74]
whereby one must assemble the 22 letters of the Hebrew alphabet
(and with appropriate head and lip movements), permute them
with the Tetragrammaton, and all the vowels
in the array of the 221 gates of meaning–

through 73 years[75] {2/(7x3): 221 gates} of a schizophonetic
poetics, obsessive letter combination and permutation
bissett is rebordering dis/orders of Abstraction,
or in Korzybskian terms, creating an interdependent heuristics
which speaks to many worlds simultaneously
and asks us to both hear and see language in new ways.

"full uv echoes," "moistyur murmerings," where "rippuling shine swet dripping," bissett reminds us how borders become a series of traces, cinders, inscribed in a spectral economy of exile, rupture and uncertainty –

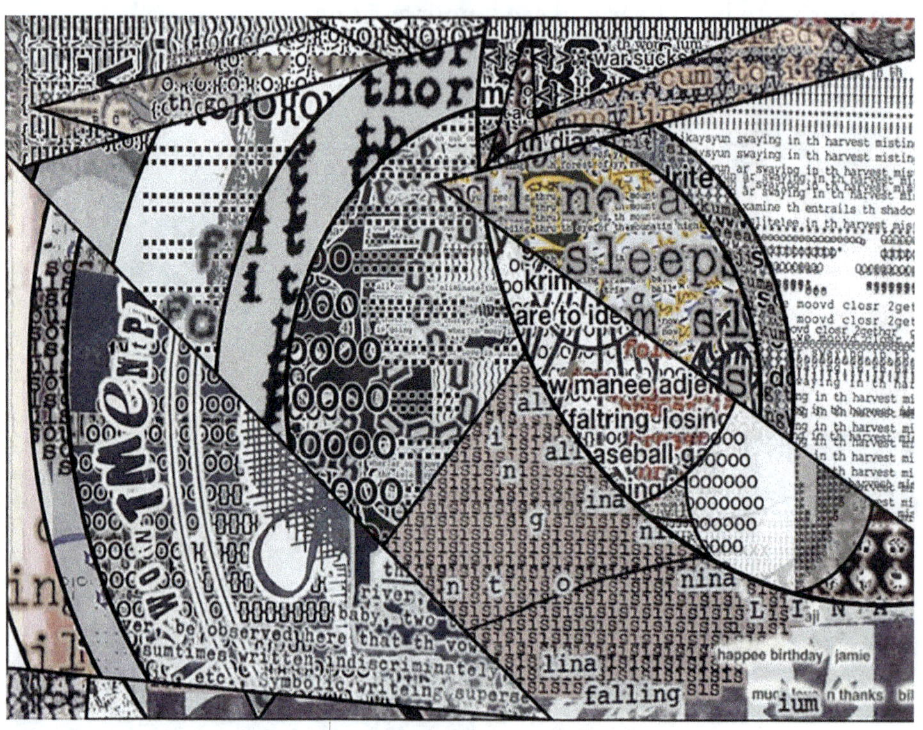

carving a "langwage" that is (in)finitely "raging," "[t]ekstatik," "vishyunary" and "sublingual," and through "a star studdid gathring uv th judgd n th judging,"[76] reminds us how *thr is / no essenshul storee so manee view points/ so manee views/ approximaysyuns*[77]

and "s[]eep inside each othr all"[78]

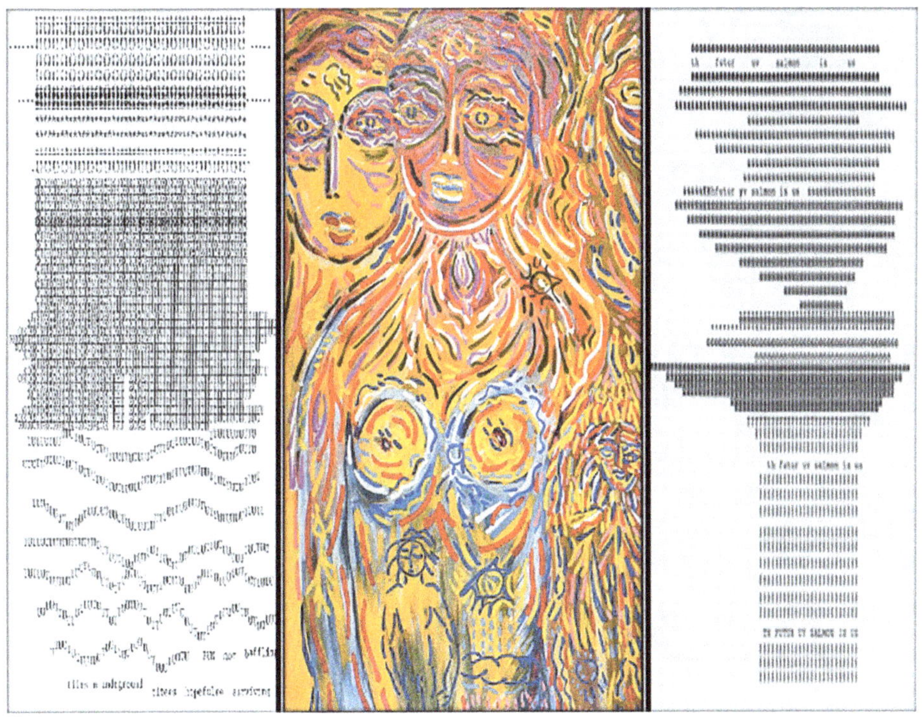

And this sense of multiplicitous subjectivity is directly synecdochic of the gaps, caesuras and silences which exist between language and all that it represents; and how even while summoning direct, physical, urgent connexion, is a constant reminder of language's inherent uncontainability.

14

In Barthesian terms, the language becomes:

a text of pulsional incidents, [a] language lined with flesh,
a text where we can hear the grain of the throat…a whole
carnal stereophony: the articulation of the tongue, not
meaning of language,[79] or for bissett, "rainbow mewsik"

(embodying within it the Hebrew word *ain* –
which contains everything and nothing simultaneously)

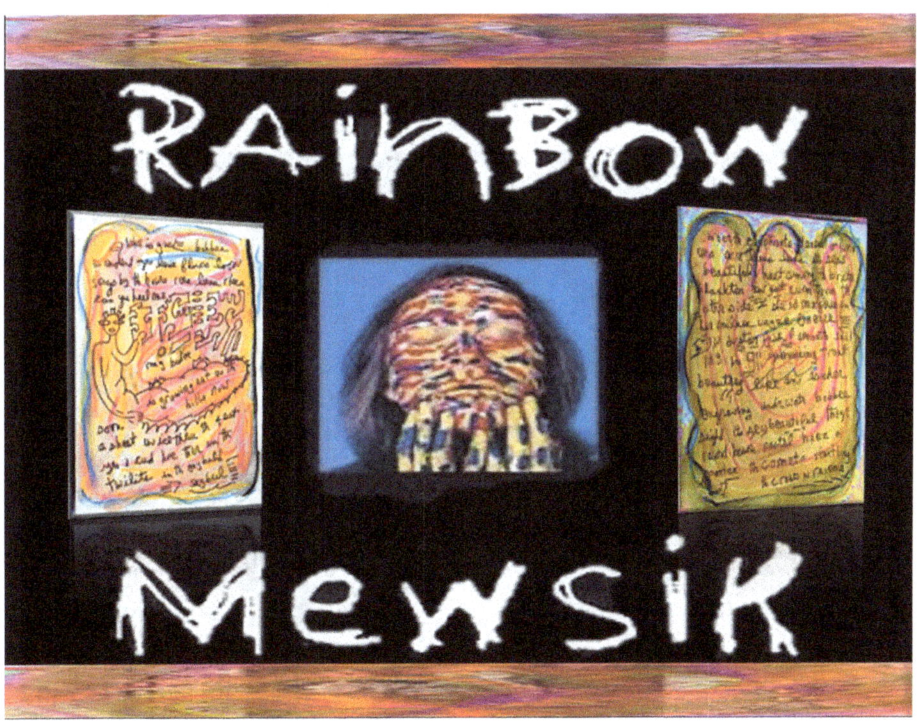

Between the nothing and the "all-ness," between time, difference, truth and meaning, bissett's idiosyncr[e]tic spelling, lack of orthogoraphy, fluid margins, *verfremdungst*-ey infusions, each page emerges as a surface of otherness where through a Jabèsian lens, we enter its warm flesh; enter it sometimes through the skin of its meaning, its form. Enter it with vigilance through its thresholds, agonies and garrulousness, through its illegibilities and dissimulation, disguises, dreams, affirmations and displacement.

Thus, between the writing and the written and the yet to be written, where all is shattered fragmented; wandering and rebellious; between borders, orders, laws, flaws, codes, idioms, territories, terrortories, deserts and promises --

questions, probes, anxieties, abandonments, absences, abscesses, obsessions and flourishes, bissett writes himself through a complex of codes, texts; logic systems saturated with palimpsestic his/herstoricities, "unprediktabiliteez," promiscuity and possibility where the meaning of meaning lies --

between "th improper" inappropriate (impropriotous, riotous), depropriated, exappropriated celebrating all that is *insani* / un-sanitized full of not "causality" but "pause-ality" and repels, re-appelles or propels itself between readability and resistance.

And as a sapirous reciprocity of paracitation, quotation, restoryation,[80] appendices which binds a range of differences and discriminations that inform the discursive and political practices of cultural hierarchization, bissett urges the listener to rethink the relation between these i.e. these dominant discursive practices, social and political lines of power and how this renegotiation of textual and sonic space becomes a powerful tool for socio-political transformation and change.

Or (to use Volosinov's terms), a "kaleidoscopic" clash of social accents, that displaces structures of authority, bissett opens up a space for new political initiatives through contemporary poetic thinking. Through a constant re-negotiation of language, power and representation, re-locating location as a location of locution a collation of illocatable occasions, a locus of interlocutory collusion, he turns the hybrid ear of the Other back onto itself --

20

and provides a political aesthetics to articulate and negotiate an unassimilable, aporetic language and history within the contingent margins of acoustic space, pre/science and sanity

Auf wider [sane]

Scenes, Screams,
Screens and Semes
The Salomaic Elasticity of
the Page and the Stage

Intro

Whether on the page or on the stage, for the last 35 years, I've been consumed with investigating language not just as a signifying medium but as a massive, multipart and global algorhythm, a celebratory praxis of pulsing plays, *appelées* (callings), pulls, plies pliés of hyper-spatial interplays; creating visceral sensoria of both material and acoustic space, acknowledging them as two separate yet mutually embracing realms of possibility, generating a contiguous infolding of meaning – highlighting how language is always *between* multiple cultures and traditions, renditions, re-coatings, re-codings courting accordance, discordance a chordal dance, dalliance, sallying through shades, shadows, shards as meaning slips between difference, appliance, appearance, negotiating how between text/sound/performance/page/stage/screen, language gets threaded through inflection, reflection, insurrection, confection, annexion and desire and how meaning's produced and reproduced intermediatically, and how that effects its message.

. . .

Forging a site of radical grafting, linkages and ludic identities, *Salomé Woman of Valor*, which is both a book and a Spoken Word Opera -- published in an English/Italian bi-lingual edition, a Bengali edition, an English-only libretto, CD *and* as a live touring Spoken Word Opera negotiates a range of aesthetic intersections – not only in the integration of styles and traditions, but how this manifests differently through the eye and in the ear.

Performed live with avant-garde middle eastern klezmer jazz musicians, dancers and vispo screen projections, it asks the viewer / listener to think about ways one both hears and receives information: How that information is always mutiperspectival and slippery; ex-statically palimpsested, celebrating the porous aporia between hearing and seeing, seeing and saying, highlighting how communication itself is always already a commune–occasion or colloquation, an illocatable locution of ludic loci.

1

Since the myth was first alluded to in the Jewish apocrypha in 14-71 AD, and in Mark and Mathew in the early 2nd C.,[81] the anti-Semitic, somewhat misogynous myth was popularized by Oscar Wilde, and cycles of powerful women have slipped into her skin over the last 2000 years – Sarah Bernhardt, Maude Allen, Mata Hari, Little Egypt, Ida Rubenstein, Alla Nazimova and Collette --

exposing how, transgressive and subversive, textually and performatively, Salomé not only threatens the social order of civilized behavior but exposes how language, meaning and symbology shift over time in conjunction with the zeitgeist; aesthetic, political and social orders of the day -- and through space-time contingencies are re-staged through the re-invention of tradition and history; re-orienting her story, her language and her meaning through both textual and performative spaces.[82]

3

In Korzybskian terms, not only binding time,[83] but binding high and low culture; the music hall and the circus, the sacred secularity of eroticisim religiosity academic discourse, French feminist theory, kabbalah, midrash, the lexicon and rhythms of pop culture, klezmer, jazz, bhangra -- where textuality, visuality, orality simultaneously erupt as a Mystery Play, a Miracle Play, a Morality Play, A Carnival Play -- a palimpsestic web of echopoeic referents, underscoring how meaning-making *is always* an anti-hegemonic *dance* of signification.

4

& sAyS:
DanCe foR Me SaLoMÉ JuSt dAnCe
FOr RHyThM iS a DAnCeR,

a PRiVaTe DaNcEr, RAin DaNcEr moOnDaNCe,
sALOmé yOu ArE tHe DaNcInG QuEeN
DAnCe nOw SAlOmÉ COmE
dAnciNg In tHe nIgHt oF thE dAnCiNg fLaMe DaNcinG
oN tHe CeiLiNg, iN tHe DArK, JuSt pUt On YoUr rEd sHoeS aNd dAnCe

'caUsE yOu WerE mAde for DaNciNg, DaNCiNg IN tHe STreEet
iN tHe mOoNlIgHt, sALoME dO YOu WaAnNa daNcE NoW

iN a laNd oF a 1000 DaNceS, MUsiC boX DAnCeR,
dANcE mE tO tHe EnD oF LoVe,

DaNCe oN gLasS, oN a VoLcaNO daNcE wiTh mE
aNd doN't foRgeT to daNcE, daNcE tHe NiGhT aWay
JuSt DanCe litTLe SiSteR, TiNy DaAnCer aNd SAvE tHe LaSt DaNcE fOr mE

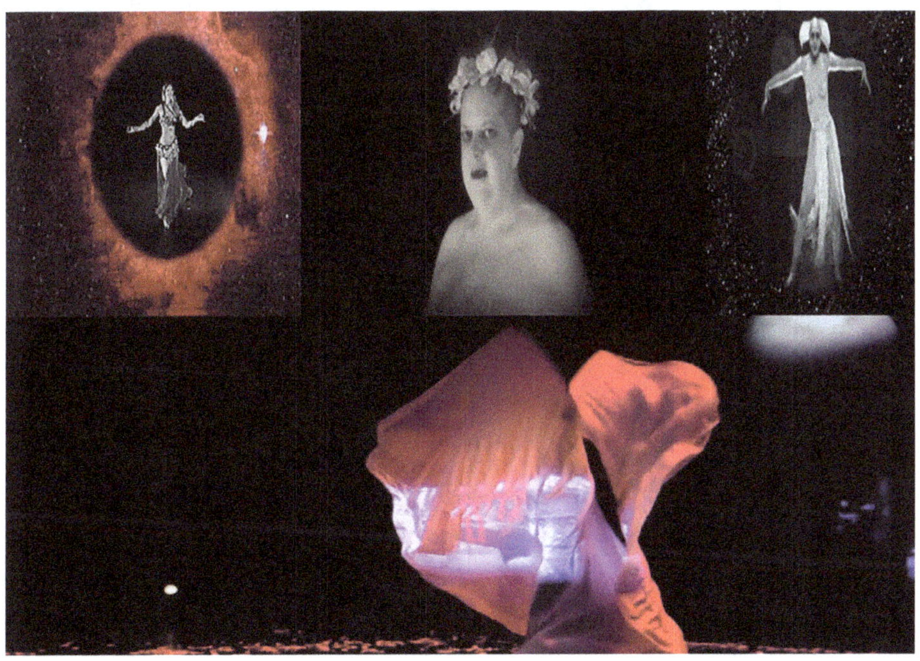

5

And like a dancing manifestation of a McLuhan mosaic, which hyper-referentially draws on and borrows from a range of intertextual periods, currents, semantic environments; intra-textatic axes of acoustic arrangements, whether on the page or on the stage, language gathers into a countersignative contract which tracks and re-tracks, contracts into an ever-expansive realm of possibility and enunciation --

"a hubub of sensation" where as much as what is revealed is concealed. And as per Watzlawick's, language cannot *not* communicate," through both medium, message, map, territory; language and meaning explode as an intertextilic web of "abstraction."

Blurring borders, orders, laws, mirrors, screens, walls; through a caterwaulery of lolling scrolls brawling sprawls of extracted maculates bracketed tracks, hacked fractures -- as in any mosaic, as much as what is revealed is concealed. And language becomes 'paint', all fragmented, palimpsested, bifurcated highlighting the construction of memory, the materiality of language and the ever-recombinatory swirling nature of meaning production; foregrounding how language is always-already intertextatically layered and proprioceptively received -- where seductive swathes of texture, sound, typographies synecdochic of how meaning unveils itself as an ever-spiraling space where "Origin" is unlocatable; and everything's a re-articulation of a re-articulation, erupting in an irrepresentable present non present or resonant present that continually escapes itself.

8

And, as the myth goes, the dance Salomé dances is the dance of the 7 *veils*; avails the veil of the veil unveiling (value volés, valor *voile* voici voila!), exposing how language and meaning are always both a literal and figural intertextilic web of obfuscation[84].

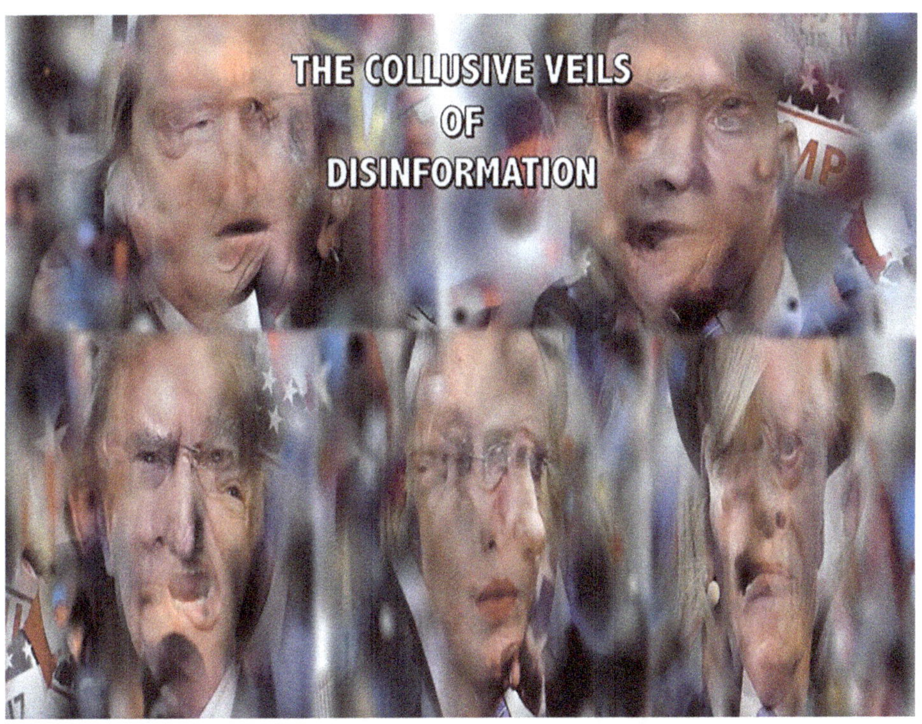

Concealing but penetrable, opaque, translucent and diaphanous, veils allow light (knowledge, meaning), to be filtered through threads, building illusion while implying truth: Allow for fantasy and mystery unveiling how and where truth *lies*: in a vexed nexus of infected lex, where facts refracted as facts in flux. Thus, Salomé's dance is a profound tear in these veils of concealment.

10

Whether it's John the Baptist, veiling his love for Salomé, Oscar Wilde veiling his homosexuality, Maude Allen veiling her sordid family history (her beloved brother, a convicted pedophile necrophiliac), or Mata Hari veiling her lowly Dutch heritage and secret life as a German spy, veiling and unveiling re-voicing the voiceless, epoch after epoch, Salomé signifies how language and meaning are literally and figuratively woven patterns –

where for example, 7 unveils:

7 words in the first verse of the Torah 7 days, weeks of counting of the omer. Sitting *Shiva* 7 days shaking 7 species 7 directions in the world. Visited by 7 guests in the *Sukkah*, 7 by 7 handbreadths. And dance 7 circles on *Simchas Torah*, and on the 7th day, *mi-shabbos le-shabbos*,[85] 7 holidays, branches and blessings as the bride circles the groom 7 times called to the Torah, 7 Noachide Laws, notes, seas, spirits, stars, 7 days of cleanliness, of preparation for the construction of the *Mishkan* in the desert. And how one winds the Tefillin 7 times binding yourself to the Law 7 days of plagues, of prayers, 7 cows and stalks of grain / 7 levels of heaven, continents, *sefirot*, 7 sparks of light, 7 gates of entry for 7 female prophets

Dancing across eras and epochs, whereby (in Korzybskian terms) the present is augmented and transmitted to a future through a past that repeats itself (increasing arithmetically and advancing geometrically), or for Derrida, how with continuous proliferation, mutation and contamination, "one can no longer count its offspring or interests, its supplements or surplus values," (in)finitely divisible, porous, permeable and indeterminate, Salomé's cyclic reappearance over time points to how identity remains a *septeneral* secret within a secret that only another secret can reveal. And language as both material and acoustic, becomes a literal dance of veils.

13

A play of interwoven light, darkness, shade. For, as outlined in the sacred 13th C. Kabbalistic texts, The *Sefer Yetzirah* (*The Book of Creation*) and the *Sefer ha-Bahir*, *The Book of Illumination*, the world was created from language, white light on black light, the oral and the written simultaneous enfolding text into sound into light and though the letters enshrouded in darkness, this darkness is a manifestation of light.

14

Through light and darkness, the linking of modalized presents, referents, cycles and media environments, Salomé, like language itself becomes a cipher of recurrence gathered across hysterical boundaries. Through irony and subversion; all multiplicitous, heterogenous and contingent, and signifies a virtual compendium of perversions.

'cause, if we really think about our love affair with language and meaning, is marked by cycles of censorship and subversion, incest, fetishisms, vampirism and (with a shout-out to McLuhan's Tetrad), a little necrophilia. All to say, reading Salomé in this way, through the geo-political hybridity of media ecologic economies of power, gender; inscribed as an interstitial multilingual complex of socio-historical cultures and codes, reminds us how language itself…

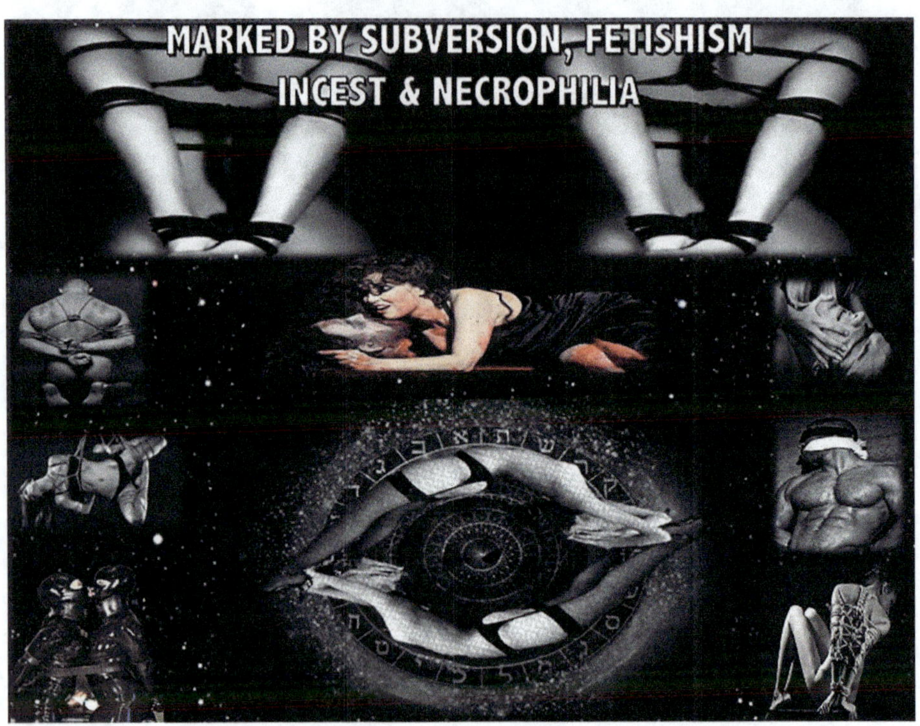

is always-already a site of repetition and re-inscription, phantomatic projection, introjection, infinitely simulacric; and synecdochic of the very condition of iteration in the negotiation of cultural formation -- a palimpsestic abscess of insouciant insistence which assembles, dissembles in a moving ensemble of resemblance, a resonant present re-presented as porous, possible and prescient, *re-processing what we say* and *how we see* and most of all ways of hearing between the oral and the written, the meme, the seme, the seen and the scream, endlessly feeding off each other.[86]

Notes

1. Derrida, Jacques, *On Touching, Jean-Luc Nancy*, trans. Christine Irizarry, Stanford University Press, California, 2005, p.12.

2. ibid. Similarly, according to Batailles, sex is our only true response to the anguish of death. Making love makes us forget that life is always on the verge of ending and that the body itself belongs just as much to death as to life. Making love recalls us to death insofar as death is only conceived on the basis of life, and indeed that is what makes it always unreal to us; what fascinates us in death is its total opacity. Until the end we think within life, with death but outside of death. Sex holds me at the edge of the certainty that one day I will disappear. And so does the telephone. See *Eroticism, Death and Sensuality*, trans. Mary Dalwood, City Lights Books, San Francisco, 1986.

3. [H]e must turn his own unconscious like a receptive organ towards the transmitting unconscious of the patient. He must adjust himself to the patient as a telephone receiver is adjusted to the transmitting microphone. Sigmund Freud, "Recommendations to Physicians Practicing Psychoanalysis" in *The Standard Edition of the Complete Psychological Works of Sigmund Freud, Volume XII* (1911-1913): Random House, New York, 2001.

4. See Derrida, *The Gift of Death*. Trans. David Wills. University of Chicago Press, 1995. In the economy of the gift, if the gift is given with no giver, then in one sense, the receiver is also the giver, or "caller".

5. Claude Shannon's communication theory points out how entropy means there's always noise in the system, how something always gets lost in transmission.

6. Proust, M. *Remembrance of Things Past*, Col. I. New York: Vintage Books, 1983.

7. As both McLuhan and Carpenter point out, the word "phony" means "unreal voice."

8. Kern, Stephen. *The Culture of Time and Space: 1880-1918*. Cambridge: Harvard University Press, 1983, p.69.

9. As Bruce Sterling points out in his introduction to *The Hacker Crackdown: Law and Disorder on the Electronic Frontier* (Bantam Books, New York, 1993), "Cyberspace is the "place" where a telephone conversation appears to occur. Not inside your actual phone, the plastic device on your desk. Not inside the other person's phone, in some other city. The place between the phones. [...] in the past twenty years, this electrical "space," which was once thin and dark and one-dimensional—little more than a narrow speaking-tube, stretching from phone to phone—has flung itself open like a gigantic jack-in-the-box. Light has flooded upon it, the eerie light of the glowing computer screen. This dark electric netherworld has become a vast flowering electronic landscape. Since the 1960s, the world of the telephone has cross-bred itself with computers and television, and though there is still no substance to cyberspace, nothing you can handle, it has a strange kind of physicality now. It makes good sense today to talk of cyberspace as a place all its own."

10. *phoinikeia grammata*

11. Like how in *Shibboleth,* (in *Acts of Literature,* trans. David Attridge, Routledge, 1992), Derrida talks about circumcision: as the cut that opens the word or the heart or the ear to the other; is both a cutting off and into; new communities. Thus, the telephone represents the cut that opens the space into a philophenemic network of otherness.

12. A Japanese Company, Chaku Perfume, now offers an app called Chat Perf which is designed to smell smells via iPhone. At attachment made up of an atomizer and a smell tank fits into an iPhone's dock port.

13. As Eric McLuhan points out, "the crowd of electrified nomads has no natural boundaries: it o'erleaps all natural and physical limitations. It is exempt from natural law" in "Media Ecology & the New Nomads," *Proceedings of the Media Ecology Association,* Volume 8, 2007.

14. McLuhan, Marshall. *Understanding Media.* Cambridge: MIT Press, 1994. 269.

15. Flichy, Patrice. *Dynamics of Modern Communication.* London: Sage Publications, 1995, p.82.

16. Carly Rae Jepson's, 2012, hit single https://www.youtube.com/watch?v=fWNaR-rxAic

17. Derrida, "Ulysses Gramaphone Hear Say Yes in Joyce" in *Acts of Literature.* Ed. Derek Attridge, London and New York, Routledge, 1991.

18. Ronell, Avital. *The Telephone Book: Technology, Schizophrenia, Electric Speech.* Lincoln: University of Nebraska Press, 1989.

19. Requoted from *Eidetic Traces*, Catherine Borders, https://eidetictraces.wordpress.com/tag/helene-cixous/.

20. See Rihanna's, 2016, "Work" feat. Drake. https://www.youtube.com/watch?v=HL1UzIK-flA

21. See Jean-Paul Sartre, *The Imaginary: A Phenomenological Psychology of the Imagination*, Trans. Kenneth Williford and David Rudrauf, Routledge, New York, 2013.

22. In contemporary slang, that which is "fancy" is said to be "*so extra*". Thus, the "fancy" ("imagination") should be re-negotiated through jouissance, pleasure, excess. The original presentation of this text featured a video clip of Iggy Azalea's, 2014, "Fancy" https://www.youtube.com/watch?v=O-zpOMYRi0w.

23. Marshall McLuhan, *Understanding Media*.

24. Liberally adapted from Artaud, Antonin, *The Truth and its Double*. Trans. Mary Canline Richards, New York: Grove Press, 1958.

25. Middle English (formerly also as *ingine*): from Old French *engin*, from Latin *ingenium* 'talent, device,' from *in-* 'in' + *gignere* 'beget'; ingenius. The original sense was 'ingenuity, cunning' (surviving in Scots as *ingine*), hence 'the product of ingenuity, a plot or snare'.

26. Johanna Drucker, drawing on Matthew Kirschenbaum's distinction between "phenomenological materiality'" and the "ontological immateriality" of the electronic text: "the visual form of the letter on the screen [is] fully material… even though the 'letter' exists as a stored sequence of binary digits with no tactile, material apparency to it in that fundamental condition." Johanna Drucker, "Intimations of Immateriality: Graphical Form, Textual Sense, and the Electronic Environment" in *Reimagining Textuality: Textual Studies in the Late Age of Print*. Ed. Elizabeth Bergmann Louiseaux and Neil Fraistat, Madison. University of Wisconsin Press, 2002.

27. Hegel, *The Phenomenology of Spirit*. Trans. Arnold V. Miller, J N. Findlay, and Johannes Hoffmeister. Oxford: Clarendon Press, 1979.

28. The Zohar speaks of the Torah as being a blueprint to the world, implying that even before the world as we know it, there was a prototype. Further according to the *Bahir*, the world was always already in perpetual recurrence: "Rabbi Berachiah said:/What is the meaning of verse (Genesis 1:3), And G-d said, 'Let there be light', and there was light? Why does the verse not say, And it was so?// What is this like? A king had a beautiful object. He put it away until he had a place for it, and then he put it there. // It is therefore written,

'Let there be light, and there was light.' This indicates that it already existed."
Zohar II:151b, trans. Harry Sperling and Maurice Simon, New York: Soncino
Press, 1984.

29. *Profiles of the Future: An Inquiry into the Limits of the Possible*, Harper and
Rowe: NY, 1962.

30. Telepathy (from the Ancient Greek *tele* meaning "distant" and *pathos* meaning
"feeling, perception, passion, experience"), is the transmission of information
from one person to another without using any of our known sensory
channels or physical interaction. The term was coined in 1882 by the classical
scholar Frederic W. H. Myers.

31. With the idea originating in 1753, it was often referred to as the "spirit-
telegraph," the electromagnetic telegraph seemed possessed as it
"miraculously" transmitted messages instantaneously over long distances.

32. "[G]enuine aura appears in all things, not just in certain kinds of things, as
people imagine." Walter Benjamin, "Protocols of Drug Experiments," *On
Hashish*, trans. Howard Eiland et al., Cambridge, Mass., 2006.

33. Aura Dolls, North America's, first sex doll brothel features these "sex robots".
Located in Mississauga, Canada, servicing customers with "the world's most
beautiful silicone ladies." See Image 17.

34. See George Herbert Mead, *Mind, Self, and Society*, ed. C.W. Morris, University
of Chicago Press: Chicago, 1934.

35. As outlined in the earliest Kabbalistic mystical text, the *Sefer Yetzirah*, Book
of Formation or Book of Creation (which uncannily was also   received by
early commentators as a treatise on mathematical and linguistic theory).

36. See Idel, Moshe. *Golem: Jewish Magical and Mystical Traditions on the Artificial
Anthropoid*. State University of New York Press, 1990. Also, Faye Levine,
Practical Kabbalah, http://kabbalah.fayelevine.com/golem/pk008.php.
Throughout history there are many instances of Golems. Rabbi Yehuda
Loew, the Marharal of Prague, used his golem Yosele (a.k.a. Yosef, Joseph)
to protect the Jews of his community, who were under constant threat of
slander and attack from the local Christians, who believed the Jews killed
Christian children and used their blood in rituals, or to make Passover
matzot. This is naturally absurd, not just for the obvious reasons, but because
the handling and use of blood is forbidden by kosher laws. Yosele was sent to
patrol the Jewish quarter of Prague, on the lookout for wrongdoers; he rooted
out evidence against the people trying to frame the Jews for murder; he
helped round up sinners; he assisted the rabbi in investigations. It was only

when Emperor Rudolf II decreed there would be no more blood libels against the Jews and Thaddeus, the primary instigator of the accusations, had been discredited, that Rabbi Loew deactivated Yosele. The golem's clay remains in the attic of the synagogue, which was then proclaimed off-limits.

Golems have also been used to temporarily raise the dead. A number of stories exist in which a person is brought back to life by undergoing a ritual similar to the creation of a golem, which culminates in a Name of God being written on the deceased's arm, or having a paper bearing the Name put into their mouth. This was only done under dire circumstances; for example, if the dead person could do something or provide information which would save an innocent life. When the task is done, the Name is removed, and the body instantly collapses, either suddenly decomposed or turning to dust.

37. According to an interview in Variety, Jan. 31, 2014 with Dag Kittlaus, *co-founder and former CEO of Siri (which he sold to Apple in 2010*: "Back in 2007, when my co-founders and I created Siri, we were trying to build the world's first true virtual personal assistant, to make interacting with your devices as simple as a conversation. Siri was built to get things done."

38. Donna Harraway, "A Cyborg Manifesto, Science, Technology and Socialist-Feminism in the Late Twentieth Century" in *Simians Cyborgs and Women: The Reinvention of Nature*, New York: Routledge, 1991. Further, with the de-fetishization of the body (in any traditional sense), technology reminds us of our increasingly intense connection to all things; animate and non-animate. Highlighting the very mystical (Kabbalistic) view that every nook, book, pad, pod, surface all vibrates internally; is imbued and pulsing with inter-connected energy.

39. Borrowed from a phrase of Antonin Artaud (from the *Theatre of Cruelty*), Deleuze and Guattari's, "body without organs" describes the virtual dimension of the body and, ultimately, the basic substratum of reality. Nov. 1947: How Do You Make Yourself a Body Without Organs?" In *A Thousand Plateaus: Capitalism and Schizophrenia*. Trans. Brian Massumi. Minneapolis: University of Minnesota Press, 1987. "You never reach the Body without Organs, you can't reach it, you are forever attaining it, is a limit. People ask, So what is this BwO?—But you're already on it, scurrying like a vermin, groping like a blind person, or running like a lunatic; desert traveler and nomad of the steppes. On it we sleep, live our waking lives, fight—fight and are fought—seek our place, experience untold happiness and fabulous defeats; on it we penetrate and are penetrated; on it we love...," p.150.

40. "That is to say, desire and *jouissance* are inherently antagonistic, exclusive even: desire's *raison d'etre* (or "utility function," to use Richard Dawkins's term) is not to realize its goal, to find full satisfaction, but to reproduce itself

as desire." Slavoj Zizek. Desire: Drive = Truth: Knowledge. See *Umbr(a): Identity and Identification*, Center for Psychoanalysis and Culture; Buffalo, 1998, pp. 147-152.

41. Walter Benjamin, *On Hashish*.

42. The development of autonomous technology is also explored in Abigail Child's award winning 2020 documentary, *Origin of the Species* where through extensive research conducted in cutting edge laboratories in Japan and the US, such as Terasem Movement Foundation, Hanson Robotics, Tuft Human-Robot Interaction Lab, FuRo, CharmLab and Realbotix, exposes some of the mind-blowing advancements and ethical concerns in the contemporary world of android development.

43. "I call this peculiar form of self-hypnosis Narcissis narcosis, a syndrome whereby man remains us unaware of the psychic and social effects of his new technology as a fish of the water it swims in. As a result, precisely at the point where a new media-induced environment becomes all pervasive and transmogrifies our sensory balance it also becomes invisible." Marshall McLuhan, "The Playboy Interview," 1961. Also as discussed in *Understanding Media: The Extensions of Man*, "the youth Narcissus mistook his own reflection in the water for another person. This extension of himself by mirror numbed his perceptions until he became the servomechanism of his own extended or repeated image. The nymph Echo tried to win his love with fragments of his own speech, but in vain. He was numb. He had adapted to his extension of himself and had become a closed system.

44. Pound, Ezra. ABC of Reading. New York: New Directions, 1934, p.73.

45. McLuhan, Marshall. *Understanding Media: The Extensions of Man*. Similarly, in his Playboy interview, when asked why should it be the artist rather than the scientist who perceives these relationships and foresees these trends? He answers, "Because inherent in the artist's creative inspiration is the process of subliminally sniffing out environmental change. It's always been the artist who perceives the alterations in man caused by a new medium, who recognizes that the future is the present, and uses his work to prepare the ground for it. But most people, from truck drivers to the literary Brahmins, are still blissfully ignorant of what the media do to them; unaware that because of their pervasive effects on man, it is the medium itself that is the message, not the content, and unaware that the medium is also the massage — that, all puns aside, it literally works over and saturates and molds and transforms every sense ratio. The content or message of any particular medium has about as much importance as the stenciling on the casing of an atomic bomb. But the ability to perceive media-induced

extensions of man, once the province of the artist, is now being expanded as the new environment of electric information makes possible a new degree of perception and critical awareness by nonartists," "The Playboy Interview: Marshall McLuhan," *Playboy Magazine,* March 1969.

46. Marshall McLuhan, "Introduction to *The Bias of Communication,* Harold A. Innis, 1951, vol. 8 of *Marshall McLuhan—Unbound*, introduction by W. Terrence Gordon, Corte Madera, CA: Gingko Press, 2005, p.5.

47. With antecedents in the Duchampian readymade, 80s appropriation art, Brazilian concrete poetry, and French Oulipian constraint writing. In France, "poetic documents" work as site-specific nodes of sociological and linguistic analyses; in the Philippines, conceptualism serves as performative institutional critique. Sweden and Chile have 40-year legacies of conceptual writing born of disparate political climates and their critiques. In Iran, literary appropriation is literary tradition; current Russian videopoetics has its roots in 1970s Moscow Conceptualism. Conceptual writing is newer to Germany and Mexico, where practitioners use its techniques to rearticulate contemporary and past history.

48. Kittler, Friedrich, *A Discourse Networks 1800/1900*. Stanford, Calif.: Stanford University Press, 1990, 250. And as Johanna Drucker points out in "Understanding Media, Craig Dworkin's `No Medium'" Los Angeles Review of Books, July 9, 2013, Kittler opens up a dialogue between theories of media and poetic artistic experimental practices.

49. According to Kenny Goldsmith, "it employs...uncreativity, unoriginality, illegibility, appropriation, plagiarism, fraud, theft, and falsification as its precepts; information management, word processing, databasing, and extreme process as its methodologies; and boredom, valuelessness, and nutritionlessness as its ethos. Language as junk, language as detritus. Nutritionless language, meaningless language, unloved language, *entartete sprache*, everyday speech, illegibility, unreadability, machinistic repetition. Obsessive archiving & cataloging, the debased language of media & advertising; language more concerned with quantity than quality.

50. Single letters are 50 cents and single words are 1 dollar.

51. Or more aptly, "information ecology." According to Lance Strate in "Containers, Computers and the Media Ecology of the City," "this phrase appears as part of the Summary Minutes of a meeting of the United States Advisory Council on the National Information Infrastructure, and .... Kapor used the term in an argument over appropriate metaphors, and as an alternative to the "information superhighway." Interestingly, "information

ecology" has also been used by Reagan's FCC director, Mark Fowler: "as the ecological system has deteriorated, I think the man-made information ecology--the ebb and flow of words, voice, data--has vastly improved, so that we now live in a world more tightly bound, more in touch one part with another, than at any other moment in history." See "Containers, Computers, and the Media Ecology of the City." *media ecology*, 1 [online] 1996, pp. 1-13 https://web.archive.org/web/19990218060103/http://raven.ubalt.edu/features/media_ecology/articles/96/strate1/strate_1.html

52. And if an "environment is process, not container" (McLuhan and Parker), the container is never separate from its contents. In a process of endless repetition and transcription, within Conceptual Poetry, the contents generate contents, plays out as an autopoietic system."

53. Ezra Pound, *ABC of Readings*, New Directions: New York, 1960, p.29.

54. Seeing "the great newspaper" as a synthesis of a day in the world's life, F. T. Marinetti, "Destruction of Syntax—Imagination without Strings Words-in-Freedom 1913," trans. R. W. Flint, in *Futurist Manifestoes*, ed. Umbro Apollino, trans. Robert Brain, R. W. Flint, J. C. Higgitt, Caroline Tisdall from *Documents of 20th Century Art*, ed. Robert Motherwell, The Viking Press, New York, 1973), p.96.

55. With this project, Goldsmith coined the term "Uncreative Writing", seeing uncreativity as a constraint-based process. News as a fleeting moment concretized, captured, then reframed into the discourse of literature.

56. See Walter Benjamin, "Ninth Thesis on the Philosophy of History", "A Klee drawing named 'Angelus Novus'" shows an angel looking as though he is about to move away from something he is fixedly contemplating. His eyes are staring, his mouth is open, his wings are spread. This is how one pictures the angel of history. His face is turned toward the past. Where we perceive a chain of events, he sees one single catastrophe that keeps piling ruin upon ruin and hurls it in front of his feet. The angel would like to stay, awaken the dead, and make whole what has been smashed. But a storm is blowing from Paradise; it has got caught in his wings with such violence that the angel can no longer close them. The storm irresistibly propels him into the future to which his back is turned, while the pile of debris before him grows skyward. This storm is what we call progress." *Theses on the Philosophy of History*, *https://libcom.org/library/theses-concept-history-walter-benjamin*.

57. *Lingual Ladies*: https://bit.ly/3gy0Bao.

58. Influenced by Korzybski's general semantics and Shannon's information theory, Burroughs expressed the idea of seeing language as an alien entity by

saying, language is a virus from outer space.

59. Thus, the poem, in the words of Jacques Ellul, becomes "possessed by the spirit of technique...infected with "machinitis" and fabricate a system in which all language, communication and relationships all become machines," Jacques Ellul, *Humiliation of the Word*, trans. Joyce Main Hanks, Grand Rapids, MI: Eedmans, 1985, p.170.

60. Dec. 8, 2014 at the White House. Watch here: https://bit.ly/38trEzb.

61. See Charles Bernstein, "The Art and Practice of the Ordinary" in the *Attack of the Difficult Poems: Essays and Inventions*, University of Chicago Press, Chicago, 2011.

62. See *The Book of Probes*, Marshall McLuhan and David Carson, edited by Eric McLuhan and William Kuhns, Gingko Press, 2011. As Darren Wershler points out, "it was with thoughts of poets and painters: James Joyce's *Finnegans Wake*, Pound and the Cubist paintings of Pablo Picasso, that McLuhan concocted his phrase 'probes', Wershler, Darren, *Montreal Gazette*, Montreal, July 16, 2011.

63. First published in 1874, the book played a leading role in the pedagogic debate over whether English should be analyzed as if it were Latin, and thousands of copies were printed as textbooks in the last quarter of the 19th century.

64. Further, even broken down, the word "meme" comprised of me/me uncannily enacts how *a la* Benjamin or Stein, repetition is always already a reproduction, and reinforces the performative dimensions of identity; a host of messy mirroring. Resembling something it is not is ironically the paradox of McLuhan himself. For acknowledged as the "patron saint" of *Wired* magazine, the Father of technology and a futurist, Marshall McLuhan was a Conceptual poet – and always credited the poets of the modernist avant-gardes as "the real inspiration for his media studies." Marchand, Philip. *Marshall McLuhan: The Medium and the Messenger: A Biography*. MIT Press. Mass, 1998.

65. Form the French, *connaître* (to know, be familiar with) re-*connaître*, to remember or in this case re-member.

66. The "real understanding of the changes in modern communication... come mainly from the resourceful technicians among modern poets and painters" Marshall McLuhan, "Joyce, Mallarmé, and the Press," *Sweanee Review 62*, 1954: 42. So, whether its DNA with a poem embedded in it, crossed lines or headlines, by using the materials of the culture directly, and its critical reframing, Conceptualism has the utmost relevance for the "function and

effect of communication on society."

67. Neil Postman, Crazy Talk. Stupid Talk, Delta Books, Dell Publishing Company, New York, 1976. Or put in another way: "Crazy talk is, in fact, almost always characterized by simple-minded conceptions of complex relationship."

68. Slavoj Zizek, *Zizek's Jokes,* ed. Audun Morensen, MIT Press, Mass, 2014, p.57.

69. Text drawn from *Checking In* (Talonbooks, Vancouver, 2018), and also text from forthcoming *Ærotomania: The Book of Lumenations*. The original presentation was performed live accompanied by a (vispo) videopoem created in collaboration with digital media artist, Jim Andrews. Full piece can be seen here: https://bit.ly/3yclON2.

70. "Kontest Carnage" (*Geist*. Vol.12, No.50, p.78) bissett blurs the boundary between Poem, Movie Review, Political Treatise and Horror Story. And blurring notions of history and identity, in his own words: "bissett originalee from lunaria was on th first childrns shuttlfrom that planet wch is veree far away landid in halifax bcame immediatelee puzzuld by erthling wayze trying 2 hang in as muchas possibul with life on erth bgan painting erlee c. 10-11 whn i was in th oxygen tent n wasint allowd 2 dew aneething bgan writing thn as well pickd both up latr n have alwayze wantid 2 keep going on with both wundrful aktivitees alwayze wanting 2 explor image lettr shape stroke colour sound th picksyurs in th lettrs in th images in th lettrs have shown at th vancouvr art gal modern fuel selby hotel just deserts 519 london artmuseum art scene secret hand shake art galleree forest citeeart galleree most recent shows cowichan duncan art galleree bcn th rob schouten art galleree whitby island washington state" (personal correspondence).

71. Alfred Korzybski, *Science and Sanity*.

72. See Steve McCaffery, bill bissett, "A Writing Outside Writing," in *North of Intention: Critical Writings*, 1973-1986, Roof Books: New York, 2000.

73. Such as Rav Zhitomar of Prague.

74. To make a Golem, one must assemble the 22 letters of the Hebrew alphabet and permute them with the Tetragrammaton, and all the vowels, in the array of the 221 gates of meaning. Each sequence contains 442 letters, so to complete all 22 letters of the alphabet, one must use 4862 letters. Each of these letters must be pronounced with every possible combination of the 5 primary vowels and the 4 letters of the Tetragrammaton, a total of 9724 pronunciations for each lettered pair. This means the entire exercise makes use of 486,200 pronunciations. Estimating 4 syllables a second: 1½ hours per sequence resulting in 35 hours to complete the uninterrupted process

to create a Golem (my calculations from the commentary of Rabbi Eliezar Rokeach on the *Book of Formation*). However, there is also evidence that creating a Golem was primarily not only a physical procedure, but rather, a highly advanced meditative technique. By chanting the appropriate letter combination together with the letters of the Tetragrammaton, the initiate could form a very real mental image of a human being, limb by limb. Once the conceptual Golem was completed, this spiritual potential could be transferred to a clay form and actually animate it. For a translation of Eleazar of Worms' original text with an explanation, see Idel's *Golem: Jewish Magic and Mystical Traditions on the Artificial Anthropoid*. SUNY Press, 2019. For figures, tables, and a highly detailed explanation of the 221 gates, see Aryeh Kaplan's translation and commentary on the *Sefer Yetzirah*, Weiser Books: Mass, 1997.

75. Born in 1939, bissett's age at the writing of this piece.

76. bill bissett, "from th memorabul gala at orangevilee n neepor landing." *scars on th seehors* Talonbooks: Vancouver, 1999.

77. bill bissett, "(no tay syun) pome time pome staysyun" in *Open Letter*. Fifth Series, No. 2, 1982.

78. bill bissett, *we sleep inside each othr all*. Ganglia Press: Toronto, 1965.

79. Roland Barthes, *The Pleasure of the Text*. Trans. R. Miller. Hill and Wang: New York, 1975, p.49.

80. In light of "quotation" and "restoryation," many of these images draw upon the stunning vispo collaboration between Jim Andrews and bill bissett. Full project can be seen here: http://www.vispo.com/aleph3/images/bill_bissett/index.htm

81. The only historical reference that Herodias' daughter's name was Salomé is from Flavius Josephus who makes no other claims about her – not that she danced for Herod, not that she demanded John's head, but only that she went on to marry twice and live peacefully. The other apocryphal reference is that a 'daughter' danced for Herod, causing him to lose his mind and kill John the Baptist. Thus, the conflated Salomé that appears in the Wilde play, Strauss opera and all subsequent productions, is an amalgamated construct.

82. *Salomé: Woman of Valor* videopoems which were originally excerpted in this piece can be viewed here: *White Abbot*: https://bit.ly/3mzAGD4, *Dance of Desire:* https://bit.ly/38aIu5P, *Gardens of Eros*: https://bit.ly/3ymMhHz, *Drown Me:*https://bit.ly/3ksTlxo.

83. See Alfred Korzybski, *Manhood of Humanity*: The Science and Art of Human

Engineering, E.P. Dutton and Co: New York, 1921, also Lance Strate, *On The Binding Biases Of Time*, The New Non-Aristotelian Library, Institute of General Semantics, Texas, 2011.

84. Images by Jim Andrews as part of his "The Moral Deformity of Team Trump" series. http://www.vispo.com/aleph3/an.html?d=Jim%20Andrews.

85. Refers to Mishnaic law that the proper frequency of intercourse for a couple (in which the husband is a scholar) is *mi-shabbos le-shabbos*: once a week on Friday night. Also 7 is especially crucial in that for Jews, the organizing principle of time revolves around the number 7. According to Michael Wex, (*Just Say Nu,* St. Martin's Press, New York, 2007), the 7-day biblical calendar allows for shabbes, unlike the 10-day solar calendar of the Egyptians. And, it's not just the 7th day itself which is significant, but the whole 7-day period that that day defines. For example, when you say the Psalm for the day, you always begin with "*ha-yom yom X be-shabbos,*" today is day X of the *Shabbos* (7th day) of the week. Further, as outlined in Leviticus, everything goes in 7 year cycles, (As per Lev. 23:15-6), the day after the 7th day, you shall count 7 complete weeks until the day after the 7th week and after 7 7-year cycles there is a Jubilee year – where "you shall not sow, neither shall you reap... or harvest" (Lev. 25:11). Certain types of land sales are cancelled, debts are annulled, slaves who refused to leave their masters after six years go free in the 7th (Ex. 21:2). Thus, within Jewish thinking 7 represents both a sense of freedom, and the ultimate marker of time.

86. Original presentation included a clip of this video, *White Abbot*: https://bit.ly/3mzAGD4, featuring footage from Charles Bryant's, 1923 film, *Salome* and reconstructed music and lyrics of Jefferson Airplane's, "White Rabbit," enacts in both form, content, media and message, an anthopophagic rendering -- responding to the Hegelian concept of *Erinnerung,* (meaning both memory and interiorization), and how Spirit incorporates history by assimilating, by remembering its own past. According to Derrida, this assimilation acts as a kind of sublimated eating; spirit eats everything that is external and foreign, and thereby transforms it into something internal, something that is its own.

References

Artaud, A. (1958). *The Truth and its Double*. (M.C. Richards, Trans.). New York: Grove Press.

The Bahir. (1990). Attributed to Rabbi Nehunia ben haKana. (Aryeh Kaplan, Trans.). Maine: Samuel Weiser.

Barthes, R. (1975). *Pleasure of the Text*. (R. Miller, Trans.). New York: Hill and Wang.

Baudrillard, J. (1983). *Simulations*. (P. Foss, Patton, P., & Beitchman, P. Trans.). New York, NY: Semiotext(e).

Baudrillard, J. (1994). Simulacra and Simulations. (S.F. Glaser, Trans.). Ann Arbor, MI: University of Michigan Press.

Baudrillard, J. (1982). *The Ecstasy of Communication*, Cambridge, MA: MIT Press.

Batailles, G. (1986). *Eroticism, Death and Sensuality*, (M. Dalwood, Trans.). San Francisco, CA: City Lights Books.

Benjamin, W. ([1936] 2008), *The Work of Art in the Age of its Technological Reproducibility, andOther Writings on Media*, Cambridge, MA: Belknap Press of Harvard University Press.

Benjamin, W. (1940). "Ninth Thesis on the Philosophy of History." *Theses on the Philosophy of History*, https://libcom.org/library/theses-concept-history-walter-benjamin.

Benjamin, W. (1968). *Illuminations*. New York, NY: Harcourt, Brace & World.

Benjamin, W. (1978). *Reflections*. London, UK: Jonathon Cape.

Benjamin, W. (2006). *On Hashish*. (H. Eiland, Ed.). Cambridge, MA: Belknap Press, Imprint of Harvard University Press.

Bernstein, C. (2011). "The Art and Practice of the Ordinary" in the *Attack of the Difficult Poems: Essays and Inventions*. Chicago, IL: University of Chicago Press.

Bhabha, H. K. (1994) *The Location of Culture*. London: Routledge.

bissett, b. (1966). *we sleep inside each othr all*. Toronto, ON: Ganglia Press.

bissett, b. (1967). *fires in th tempul*. Vancouver, BC: Very Stone House.

bissett, b. (1968). *awake in the red desert!* Vancouver, BC: Talonbooks.

bissett, b. (1971). *nobody owns th earth*. Toronto, ON: Anansi.

bissett, b. (1971). *what fukin thery*. Vancouver, BC: blewointmentpress.

bissett, b. (1972). *th ice bag*. Vancouver: BC, blewointmentpress.

bissett, b. (1974). *medicine my mouths on fire*. Ottawa, ON: Oberon Press.

bissett, b. (1976). *th wind up tongue*. Vancouver, BC: blewointmentpress.

bissett, b. (1980). *Selected Poems: Beyond Even Faithful Legends*. Vancouver, BC: Talonbooks.

bissett, b. (1982). "(no tay syun) pome time pome staysyun" in *Open Letter*. Fifth Series, No. 2., Toronto, ON.

bissett, b. (1987). *animal uproar*. Vancouver, BC: Talonbooks.

bissett, b. (1988). *what we have*. Vancouver, BC: Talonbooks.

bissett, b. (1990). *hard 2 beleev*. Vancouver, BC: Talonbooks.

bissett, b. (1999). "from th memorabul gala at orangevilee n neepor landing". *scars on th seehors*. Vancouver: Talonbooks.

bissett, b. (2003). "Kontest Carnage" *Geist*. Vol.12, No.50.

bissett, b. (1992). *incorrect hots*. Vancouver, BC: Talonbooks.

bissett, b. (1993). *th last photo uv th human soul*. Vancouver, BC: Talonbooks.

bissett, b. (1995). *th influenza uv logik*. Vancouver, BC: Talonbooks.

bissett, b. (2000). *b leev abul char ak trs*. Vancouver, BC: Talonbooks.

bissett, b. (2001). *lunaria*. New York: Granary Books.

bissett, b. (2008). *sublingual*. Vancouver, BC: Talonbooks.

bissett, b. (2013). *hungree throat: a novel in meditaysyun*. Vancouver, BC: Talonbooks.

bissett, b. (2019). *breth / th treez uv lunaria: selektid rare n nu pomes n* drawings 1957- 2019.Vancouver, BC: Talonbooks.

Borders, C., *Eidetic Traces,* https://eidetictraces.wordpress.com/tag/helene-cixous/

Butler, J. (1989). *Troubling Discourse*. New York, NY: Routledge.

Butler, J. (1990). *Gender Trouble: Feminism and the Subversion of Identity*. New York, NY: Routledge.

Cixous, H. (1988). *Newly Born Woman*. Trans. B. Wing, Trans.). Minneapolis, MN: University of Minnesota Press.

Cixous, H. (1988). *Writing Differences: Readings for the Seminar of Hélène Cixous*. (S. Sellers. Ed). Milton Keynes: Open University Press.

Cixous, H. (1989) "The Laugh of Medusa" in *Critical Theory Since 1965*. (H. Adams & Searle, L., Trans.). Tallahassee, FL: Florida State University Press.

Cixous, H. (1993). *Three Steps on the Ladder of Writing*. (S. Cornell & Sellers, S., Trans.). New York, NY: Columbia University Press.

Clarke, A.C., (1962). *Profiles of the Future: An Inquiry into the Limits of the Possible*, New York: Harper and Rowe.

de Saussure, F. (1959). *Course in General Linguistics*. (Charles Bally & Albert Sechehaye, A. Riedlinger., Eds., W. Baskin, Trans.). New York, NY: McGraw-Hill.

Deleuze, G., & Guattari, F. (1987). *A Thousand Plateaus: Capitalism and Schizophrenia*. (B. Massumi, Trans.). Minneapolis, MN: University of Minnesota Press.

Derrida, J. (1970). "Structure, Sign, and Play in the Discourse of the Human Sciences" in *The Structuralist Controversy*. (R. Macksey & E. Donato, Eds.). Charles Village, MD: Johns Hopkins.

Derrida, J. (1976). *Of Grammatology*. (G.C. Spivak, Trans.). Charles Village, MD: John Hopkins University Press.

Derrida, J. (1978). *Writing and Difference*. (Alan Bass, Trans.). Chicago, IL: University of Chicago Press.

Derrida, J. (1980). *The Archaeology of the Frivolous: Reading Condillac*. (J.P. Leavey Jr., Trans). Lincoln, NE: University of Nebraska Press.

Derrida, J. (1981). *Disseminations*. (B. Johnson, Trans). Chicago, IL: University of Chicago Press.

Derrida, J. (1982). *Margins of Philosophy*. (A. Bass, Trans.). Chicago, IL: University of Chicago Press.

Derrida, J. (1984). *Signponge / Signsponge*. (R. Rand, Trans.). New York, NY: Columbia University Press.

Derrida, J. (1985). *The Ear of the Other*. (P. Kamuf, Trans., C. Levesque & C. McDonald, Eds.). Lincoln, NE: University of Nebraska Press.

Derrida, J. (1986). *Memoires for Paul de Man*. C. Lindsay, J. Culler, E. Cadava & P. Kamuf, Trans.). New York, NY: Columbia University Press.

Derrida J. (1986). *Glas*. (J. P. Leavey Jr. & R. Rand, Trans.). Lincoln, NB: University of Nebraska Press.

Derrida, J. (1986). "Shibboleth" in *Midrash in Literature*. (G. H. Hartman & S. Budick, Eds.). New Haven: Yale University Press.

Derrida, J. (1987). *The Post Card: From Socrates to Freud and Beyond*. (A. Bass, Trans.). Chicago, IL: University of Chicago Press.

Derrida, J. (1987) *The Truth in Painting*. (G. Bennington & I. McLeod, Trans.).

Chicago, IL: University of Chicago Press.

Derrida, J (1987). *Of Spirit: Heidegger and the Question*. (G. Bennington & R. Bowlby, Trans.). Chicago, IL: University of Chicago Press.

Derrida, J. (1991) *Cinders*. (N. Lukacher, Trans., Ed.). Lincoln, NB: University of Nebraska Press.

Derrida, J. (1992). *Given Time: I Counterfeit Money*. (P. Kamuf, Trans.). Chicago, IL: University of Chicago.

Derrida, J. (1992). "The Law of Genre", "That Dangerous Supplement" and "Ulysses Gramaphone" in *Acts of Literature*. (D. Attridge, Ed.). New York: Routledge.

Derrida, J. (1993). *Aporias*. (T. Dutoit, Trans., W. Hamacher & D.E. Wellbery, Eds.). Stanford, CA: Stanford University Press.

Derrida, J. (1994). *Specters of Marx: The State of the Debt, the Work of Mourning, and the New International*. (P. Kamuf, Trans.). New York, NY: Routledge.

Derrida, J. (1995). The *Gift of Death*. (D. Wills, Trans.). Chicago, IL: University of Chicago Press.

Derrida, J. (1995). *On the Name*. (T. Dutoit, Ed., D. Wood, J.P Leavey Jr., & I. McLeod, Trans.). Stanford, CA: Stanford University Press.

Derrida, J. (2005). *On Touching: Jean-Luc Nancy*, (C. Irizarry, Trans.). Stanford, CA: Stanford University Press.

Drucker, J. (2002). "Intimations of Immateriality: Graphical Form, Textual Sense, and the Electronic Environment" in *Reimagining Textuality: Textual Studies in the Late Age of Print*. (E. B. Louiseaux & N. Fraistat, Eds.). Madison, WI: University of Wisconsin Press.

Drucker, J. (2013). "Understanding Media, Craig Dworkin's, 'No Medium'" 09/09/13 *Los Angeles Review of Books*.

Dworkin, Craig. (2013). *No Medium*, Cambridge, MA: MIT Press.

Eliade, M. (1959). *Cosmos and History*. (W. R. Trask, Trans.). New York, NY: Harper and Row.

Ellul, J. (1985). The *Humiliation of the Word*, (J. M. Hanks, Trans.). Grand Rapids, MI: Williams B. Eerdmans.

Fischer, N. (2019). "Poetics Statement: On Meditation and Poetry" in *The Dewdrop* (V. Able, Ed.). https://thedewdrop.org/2019/01/11/norman-fischers-poetics-statement-on-meditation-and-poetry/

Flichy, P. (1995). *Dynamics of Modern Communication*. London, UK: Sage Publications.

Freud, S. (2001). "Recommendations to Physicians Practicing Psychoanalysis" in *The Standard Edition of the Complete Psychological Works of Sigmund Freud, Volume XII* (1911-1913): New York, NY: Random House.

Goldsmith, K. (2011). *Uncreative Writing: Managing Language in the Digital Age*. New York: Columbia University Press.

Habermaas, J. (1987). *The Philosophical Discourse of Modernity*. Cambridge, MA: MIT Press.

Harraway, D. (1991). "A Cyborg Manifesto, Science, Technology and Socialist-Feminism in the Late Twentieth Century" in *Simians Cyborgs and Women: The Reinvention of Nature*, New York: Routledge.

Hegel, G.W.F. (1979). *The Phenomenology of Spirit*. A.V. Miller, Findlay, J.N & J. Hoffmeister, Trans.). Oxford, UK: Clarendon Press.

Heidegger, M. (1971). "Building, Dwelling, Thinking" in *Poetry, Language, Thought*. New York: Harper and Row.

Idel, M. (1995). *Hasidism: Between Ecstasy and Magic*. Albany, NY: SUNY Press.

Idel, M. (2019). *Golem: Jewish Magic and Mystical Traditions on the Artificial Anthropoid*. Albany, NY: SUNY Press.

Idel, M. (1989). *Language, Torah and Hermeneutics in Abraham Abulafia*. (M. Kallus, Trans.). Albany, NY: SUNY Press.

Idel, M. (1988). *The Mystical Experience in Abraham Abulafia*. (J. Chipman, Trans.). Albany, NY: SUNY Press.

Irigaray, Luce. (1991). *Marine Lover of Friedrich Nietzsche*. (G.C. Gill Trans.). New York: Columbia University Press.

Jabès, E. (1991). *From the Book to the Book: An Edmond Jabès Reader*. (R. Waldrop, Trans. with P. Joris, A. Rudolf, & Keith Waldrop). Middleton, CT: Wesleyan University Press.

Jabès, E. (1991). *Book of Questions*. (R. Waldrop, Trans). Middleton, CT: Wesleyan University Press.

Jabès, E. (1987). *The Book of Dialogue*. (R. Waldrop, Trans). Middleton, CT: Wesleyan University Press.

Kaplan, A. (1990). *Sefer Yetzirah: The Book of Creation: In Theory and Practice*. York, Maine: Samuel Weiser.

Karasick, A. (2002). "bill bissett: A Writing *Ouside* Writing", in *bill bissett: Essays on His Works*. (L. Rogers, Ed.). Toronto, ON: Guernica.

Karasick, A (2008). Shards of Light ": A Conversation with bill bissett". (Ed. T.L. Cowan), *Canadian Theater Review*.

Karasick, A. (2013). "In My Blogal Village, Print is Hot," *The Medium is the Muse*, (L. Strate & A. Karasick, Eds.). Texas: NeoPoiesis Press.

Karasick, A. (2017). *Salomé Woman of Valor* (P. Piccolo & S. Piccoli, Trans.), Padua, IT: University of Padua Press.

Karasick, A. (2018). *Checking In*. Vancouver, BC: Talonbooks.

Karasick, A., & London, F. (2020) *Salomé: Woman of Valor CD*, New York, NY, NuJu Records.

Kern, S. (1983). *The Culture of Time and Space: 1880-1918*. Cambridge, MA: Harvard University Press.

Kittlaus, D. (2014). "Siri Co-Creator Ponders the Future of the 'Her' Operating System." *Variety*. https://variety.com/2014/digital/news/siri-her-movie-spike-jonze-1201078643/

Kittler, F. (1990). *A Discourse Networks 1800/1900*. Stanford, CA.: Stanford University Press.

Korzybski, A. (1993). *Science and Sanity: An Introduction to non-Aristotelian Systems and General Semantics* (5th ed.). Englewood Cliffs, NJ: The International Non-Aristotelian Library/Institute of General Semantics. Original work published 1933.

Korzybski, A. (1994). *Manhood of Humanity*. New York: Institute of General Semantics.

Kristeva, J. (1984). *Revolution in Poetic Language*. (M. Waller, Trans.). New York: Columbia University Press.

Kristeva, J. (1982). *Powers of Horror: An Essay on Abjection*. (L.S. Roudiez., Trans.). New York: Columbia University Press.

Kristeva, J. (1980). *Desire in Language: A Semiotic Approach to Literature and Art*. (T. Gora, A. Jardine and L. Roudiez, Trans., L.S. Roudiez, Ed.,). New York: Columbia University Press.

Lacan, J. (1981). *The Four Fundamental Concepts of Psycho-Analysis*. (A. Sheridan, Trans., J-A Miller, Ed.). New York: Norton and Company.

Lamberti, Elena. (2012). *Marshall McLuhan's Mosaic: Probing the Literary Origins of Media Studies*, Toronto, ON: University of Toronto Press.

Levinas, E. (1989). *The Levinas Reader*. (S. Hand, Trans.). Oxford, UK: Basil Blackwell.

Levine, F. (2000). *Practical Kabbalah*, http://kabbalah.fayelevine.com/golem/pk008.php.

Lyotard, J-F and J-L Thebaud. (1989). *Just Gaming*. (W. Godzich, Trans.). Minneapolis, MN: University of Minnesota Press.

Marchand, P. (1998). *Marshall McLuhan: The Medium and the Messenger: A Biography*. Cambridge, MA: MIT Press.

Marinetti, F.T., (1973) "Destruction of Syntax—Imagination without Strings Words-in-Freedom 1913," (R.W. Flint, Trans.). *Futurist Manifestos*, (U. Apollino,

Ed., R. Brain, R.W. Flint, J.C. Higgitt, & C. Tisdall, Trans.). *Documents of 20th Century Art*, (R. Motherwell, Ed). New York: The Viking Press.

McCaffery, S. (1987). "Language Writing: from Productive to Libidinal Economy", "Writing as a General Economy" and "Diminished Reference and the Model Reader" in *North of Intention*, Toronto, ON: Nightwoood.

McLuhan, M. and Carson, D. (2011). *The Book of Probes*. (E. McLuhan & W. Kuhns, Eds.). Santa Rosa, CA: Gingko Press.

McLuhan, E. (2007). "Media Ecology & the New Nomads." vol. 8. *Proceedings of the Media Ecology Association*.

McLuhan, M., (1969). "The Playboy Interview: Marshall McLuhan," *Playboy Magazine*.

McLuhan, M. (1951). "Introduction to *The Bias of Communication*, H. A. Innis, vol. 8 of *Marshall McLuhan—Unbound*. Corte Madera, CA: Gingko Press.

McLuhan, M. (1951). *The Mechanical Bride: Folklore of Industrial Man*. New York: Vanguard.

McLuhan, M. (1954). "Joyce, Mallarmé, and the Press," *Sweanee Review 62*.

McLuhan, M. (1962). *The Gutenberg Galaxy: The Making of Typographic Man*. New York: McGraw Hill.

McLuhan, M. (1964). *Understanding Media*: *The Extensions of Man*. New York: McGraw Hill.

McLuhan M., & Fiore, Q. (1967). *The Medium is the Massage*. Corte Madera, CA: Ginko Press.

McLuhan, M., & McLuhan, E. (1988). "Laws of Media". *ETC: A Review of General Semantics* 34(2), 173-179.

Mead, G. H. (1934). *Mind, Self, and Society*, (C.W. Morris, Ed.). Chicago, IL: University of Chicago Press.

Ong, W.J. (1967). *The Presence of the Word*. New Haven, CT: Yale University Press.

Postman, N. (1976). *Crazy Talk. Stupid Talk*, New York: Delta Books, Dell Publishing Company.

Postman, N. (1985). *Amusing Ourselves to Death*. New York: Viking.

Postman, N. (1992). *Technopoly: The Surrender of Culture to Technology*. New York: Alfred A. Knopf.

Pound, E. (1934). *ABC of Reading*. New York: New Directions.

Proust, M. (1983). *Remembrance of Things Past*. Vol. I. New York: Vintage Books.

Ronnell, A. (1989). *The Telephone Book: Technology, Schizophrenia, Electric Speech*. Lincoln, NE: University of Nebraska Press.

Sartre, J-P. (1948). *Politics and Literature*. London. UK: Calder and Boyars.

Sartre, J-P. (2013). *The Imaginary: A Phenomenological Psychology of the Imagination*. (K. Williford & D. Rudrauf, Trans.). New York: Routledge.

Scholem, G. (1961). *Major Trends in Jewish Mysticism*. New York: Schocken.

Shannon, C. E. & Weaver. W. (1949), *The Mathematical Theory of Communication*, Urbana: University of Illinois Press.

Sterling, B. (1993). *The Hacker Crackdown: Law and Disorder on the Electronic Frontier*, New York: Bantam Books.

Strate, L. (1996). "Containers, Computers, and the Media Ecology of the City." *Media Ecology*, 1 [online] pp. 1-13

Strate, L. (2006). *Echoes and Reflections: On Media Ecology as a Field of Study*. Cresskill, NJ: Hampton Press.

Strate, L. (2011). *On the Binding Biases of Time and Other Essays on General Semantics and Media Ecology*. Fort Worth, TX: Institute of General Semantics.

Strate, L. (2014). *Amazing Ourselves to Death: Neil Postman's Brave New World Revisited*. New York: Peter Lang.

Strate, L. (2017). *Media Ecology: An Approach to Understanding the Human Condition*. New York: Peter Lang.

Stein, G. (1937). *Everybody's Autobiography*. New York: Alfred A. Knopf.

Watzlawick, P., J.B. Bavelas, & Jackson, D. D. (1967). *Pragmatics of Human Communication: A Study of Interactional Patterns, Pathologies, and Paradoxes*, New York: Norton.

Wershler, D. (2011). "The Buzz About McLuhan," 16/07/11. *Montreal Gazette*.

Wex, M. (2007). *Just Say Nu*. New York: St. Martin's Press.

Whorf, B. L. (1956), *Language, Thought and Reality*, Cambridge, MA: MIT Press.

Wolfson, E.R. (1992). *Circle in the Square: Studies in the Use of Gender in Kabbalistic Symbolism*. Albany, NY: SUNY Press.

Zizek, S. (1992). *The Sublime Object of Ideology*. London, UK: Verso.

Zizek, S. (1998). "Desire: Drive = Truth: Knowledge." *Umbr(a): Identity and Identification*, Buffalo, NY: Center for Psychoanalysis and Culture.

Zizek, S. (2014). *Zizek's Jokes*. (A. Morensen, Ed.). Cambridge, MA: MIT Press.

The Zohar. (Vols. 1-5) (1983). (H. Sperling & M. Simon, Trans.), New York: Paulist Press.

About the Author

Adeena Karasick, Ph.D, is a New York based Canadian poet, performer, cultural theorist and media artist and the author of 10 books of poetry and poetics. Her Kabbalistically inflected, urban, Jewish feminist mashups have been described as "electricity in language" (Nicole Brossard), "proto-ecstatic jet-propulsive word torsion" (George Quasha), noted for their "cross-fertilization of punning and knowing, theatre and theory" (Charles Bernstein), "a twined virtuosity of mind and ear which leaves the reader deliciously lost in Karasick's signature 'syllabic labyrinth'" (Craig Dworkin); "demonstrating how desire flows through language, an unstoppable flood of allusion (both literary and pop-cultural), word-play, and extravagant and outrageous sound-work." (Mark Scroggins). Most recently is *Checking In* (Talonbooks, 2018) and *Salomé: Woman*

of Valor (University of Padova Press, Italy, 2017), *Salomé: Woman of Valor CD*, (NuJu Records, 2020), and *Salomé Birangona*, Boibhashik (Prokashoni Press, Kolkata, 2020). Karasick teaches Literature and Critical Theory for the Humanities and Media Studies Dept. at Pratt Institute, is Poetry Editor for *Explorations in Media Ecology*, Associate International Editor of *New Explorations: Studies in Culture and Communication*, 2021 Andrew W. Mellon Foundation Award recipient and winner of the Voce Donna Italia award for her contributions to feminist thinking. The "Adeena Karasick Archive" is established at Special Collections, Simon Fraser University.